GW00871076

ROUGH MAGIC PRESENTS THE WORLD PREMIÈRE OF

WORDS OF ADVICE FOR YOUNG PEOPLE

BY IOANNA ANDERSON

WORDS OF ADVICE FOR YOUNG PEOPLE RECEIVED ITS WORLD PREMIÈRE
AT PROJECT ARTS CENTRE, DUBLIN, ON 20TH FEBRUARY 2004

THE PLAY WAS STAGED AS PART OF **ROUGH MAGIC IN REP**, RUNNING IN REPERTORY
WITH **TAKE ME AWAY** BY GERALD MURPHY

ROUGH MAGIC PRESENTS THE WORLD PREMIÈRE OF

WORDS OF ADVICE FOR YOUNG PEOPLE

BY IOANNA ANDERSON

DIRECTOR	**PHILIP HOWARD**
SET DESIGNER	**ALAN FARQUHARSON**
COSTUME DESIGNER	**EIMER NÍ MHAOLDOMHNAIGH**
LIGHTING DESIGNER	**JOHN COMISKEY**
COMPOSER	**LAURA FORREST-HAY**
PRODUCTION MANAGER	**MARIE BREEN**
STAGE DIRECTOR	**PAULA TIERNEY**
STAGE MANAGER	**JUSTIN MURPHY**
PROPS BUYER	**BREEGE BRENNAN**
PRODUCTION ELECTRICIAN	**JOE GLASGOW**
SOUND	**CORMAC CARROLL**
SET CONSTRUCTION	**THEATRE PRODUCTION SERVICES**
SCENIC ARTIST	**LIZ BARKER**
GRAPHIC DESIGN	**ALPHABET SOUP**
PUBLICIST	**PAUL FAHY**
MARKETING ASSISTANT	**NICOLE BRENNAN-O'DWYER**
ADMINISTRATOR	**ELIZABETH WHYTE**
PRODUCER	**LOUGHLIN DEEGAN**

CAST [IN ORDER OF SPEAKING]

RUBY	**SINÉAD MURPHY**
JACK	**FRANK LAVERTY**
DANNY	**DARRAGH KELLY**
ROB	**ANDREW BENNETT**
NORA	**GINA MOXLEY**
CLARA	**CATHY WHITE**

The performance runs for approximately two hours, including one interval.

WORDS OF ADVICE FOR YOUNG PEOPLE was commissioned and developed during the **SEEDS** new writing project, a joint initiative between Rough Magic Theatre Company and the Dublin Fringe Festival.

ROUGH MAGIC WOULD LIKE TO THANK THE FOLLOWING FOR THEIR KIND ASSISTANCE:
The Arts Council of Ireland, Katy and Kevin Anderson, Alex Johnston, Pamela McQueen, Phil Drury, Risteard Cooper, Conor Mullen, Hilary Reynolds, Sean Rocks, Ali White, Don Wycherley, Ali Curran, Kerry West, Vallejo Gantner, Scott Watson, Dublin City Council, and all the staff of Project Arts Centre.

Please note that the text of the play which appears in this volume may be changed during the rehearsal process and appear in slightly altered form in performance.

ROUGH MAGIC AND NEW WRITING

The core of Rough Magic's work is the development and production of new work for the stage. Founded in 1984, the company began by presenting Irish premières of major plays from the contemporary international scene, before beginning to commission and develop new plays from Irish writers. Throughout the nineties, the company presented plays by a number of significant writers including Declan Hughes, Gina Moxley, Donal O'Kelly and Arthur Riordan. In the early nineties, the company initiated a timely women's writing project which led to the production of plays by Pom Boyd and Paula Meehan. Six of these writers' debut plays were collected in Rough Magic: First Plays (New Island Books, 1999).

"Few companies set the stage ablaze quite like Rough Magic" Time Out

Following the establishment of a dedicated Literary Department in 2001, the company initiated the highly successful **SEEDS** project, in association with the Dublin Fringe Festival. **SEEDS** was established to seek out, encourage, enable, develop and stage new Irish writing. After a rigorous selection process, six emerging writers were chosen for commission. The six writers were Ioanna Anderson, Mark Doherty, Aidan Harney, Oonagh Kearney, Gerald Murphy and Raymond Scannell. Each writer was assigned a mentor from a group of highly experienced international directors – Mike Bradwell, Philip Howard, Wilson Milam, Conall Morrison, Jim Nolan and Max Stafford-Clark. Each play was developed over a twelve-month period, supported by workshops and private readings, and all six were presented as a series of public readings in 2002, followed by a seminar on new writing initiatives in Ireland. The **ROUGH MAGIC in REP** presentation of **Words of Advice for Young People** by Ioanna Anderson and **Take Me Away** by Gerald Murphy brings to four the number of **SEEDS** plays that have subsequently received full productions. A fifth is being considered for a possible production in 2004/2005.

Rough Magic will be initiating a new phase of the project, **SEEDS 2**, in 2004. Alongside support for emerging Irish writers, the new programme will also provide a development programme for emerging Irish directors.

"It is a measure of Rough Magic's success over the years that when it launches a new production, one automatically sits up and takes notice" Irish Times

In addition to the **SEEDS** project, Rough Magic continues to commission, develop and present new plays by leading Irish playwrights. Recent productions include **Shiver** by Declan Hughes (2003) and **Midden** by Morna Regan (Fringe First Award, Edinburgh Fringe Festival, 2001). At any one time, the company's rolling programme of new play commissions includes a diverse range of work at various stages of development, and we currently have six new pieces in progress for future production. The Literary Department also reads, discusses and responds to the many unsolicited scripts submitted for consideration, and provides feedback and encouragement to promising playwrights on an ongoing basis.

Further information on Rough Magic is available at **www.rough-magic.com**

IOANNA ANDERSON WRITER

Originally from Edinburgh, Ioanna is a graduate of Trinity College, Dublin. Now resident in Dublin, she is a founder-member of Greenlight Productions, who produced her first play, **Describe Joe**, which premièred in February 2000 and was revived for the Dublin Fringe Festival in 2000. **Describe Joe** also won an O.Z. Whitehead Award in 2000. Her second play, **Why I Hate the Circus**, was co-produced by Greenlight Productions and the Civic Theatre, Tallaght, in February 2001. She is currently working on new plays for the Abbey Theatre, Calipo Theatre Company and the Traverse Theatre, Edinburgh. During 2000/2001 Ioanna was a participant in the **SEEDS** project, a joint initiative between Rough Magic Theatre Company and the Dublin Fringe Festival, during which **Words of Advice for Young People** was workshopped and developed under the mentorship of Philip Howard of the Traverse Theatre.

PHILIP HOWARD DIRECTOR

Trained under Max Stafford-Clark at the Royal Court Theatre, London, on the Regional Theatre Young Director Scheme from 1988-90. Associate Director at the Traverse Theatre, Edinburgh from 1993-6, and Artistic Director since 1996. Productions at the Traverse include 16 world premieres of plays by David Greig, David Harrower, Catherine Czerkawska, Ronan O'Donnell, Nicola McCartney, Linda McLean, Sue Glover, Iain Heggie, Iain F MacLeod and the late Iain Crichton Smith. Fringe First awards for **Kill the Old Torture Their Young, Wiping my Mother's Arse** and **Outlying Islands**. Other productions at the Traverse include **Faith Healer** by Brian Friel, **Cuttin' a Rug** by John Byrne, **The Trestle at Pope Lick Creek** by Naomi Wallace, and, as Co-Director, **Solemn Mass for a Full Moon in Summer** by Michel Tremblay (also Barbican Centre, London). Productions elsewhere include **The Speculator** by David Greig in Catalan (Grec Festival, Barcelona), **Entertaining Mr Sloane** (Royal, Northampton) and **Something About Us** (Lyric Hammersmith Studio). Radio credits include **Being Norwegian** by David Greig (BBC Scotland).

ANDREW BENNETT ROB

This is Andrew's first appearance with Rough Magic. Other theatre credits include: **The Marriage of Figaro, Translations, The Map Maker's Sorrow, The House, Tarry Flynn, Tartuffe, Lolita** and most recently **The Wolf of Winter** (Abbey and Peacock); **Streetcar, Big Bad Woolf, Car Show, The Seagull** and **Foley** (Corn Exchange); **Early Morning** (Bedrock); **The Spanish Tragedy** (Loose Canon) and **We Ourselves** (Passion Machine). Film and television credits include **The General, David Copperfield, Saltwater, Angela's Ashes, Trí Scéal** and **Paths to Freedom.**

DARRAGH KELLY DANNY

Darragh's numerous Rough Magic appearances include **Three Days of Rain, Digging For Fire, The Way of The World, Northern Star, School For Scandal, Lady Windermere's Fan** and **Hidden Charges**. Other theatre credits include: **All My Sons, The Colleen Bawn, Give me your Answer, Do!, The Importance of Being Earnest, Macbeth, Philadelphia, Here I Come!** and **Angels in America** (Abbey); **Doldrum Bay** (Peacock); **Our Father** (Almeida, London); **Troilus and Cressida** (Oxford Stage Company); **Kiss of the Spiderwoman** (Co-Motion); **Brothers of the Brush** (The Arts Theatre, London); **The Merchant of Venice** (Riverbank) and **The Witches** (Olympia). Film and television credits include **Young Indiana Jones Chronicles, The Snapper, Ballykissangel, Ailsa, Snakes and Ladders, The General, Intermission** and **Paths to Freedom.**

FRANK LAVERTY JACK

This is Frank's first appearance with Rough Magic. Other theatre credits include: **Aristocrats, Iphigenia at Aulis, Translations, Famine, The Honeyspike, The Hamlet Project** and **The Comedy of Errors** (Abbey); **Sour Grapes, The Countess Cathleen, On The Inside/On The Outside, Silverlands, The Winter Thief** and **Away Alone** (Peacock); **Philadelphia, Here I Come!, A Skull In Connemara, At the Black Pig's Dyke, Song of the Yellow Bittern** and **Silverlands** (Druid); **The Dead School** (Macnas); **The Colleen Bawn** (Royal Exchange, Manchester) and **Jacko** (Yew Theatre Company). Film and television credits include: **On Home Ground** and **Glenroe** (RTÉ); **The Abduction Club** (Pathè/Samson); **Rebel Heart** (BBC NI); **The Closer You Get** (Donegal Films); **The General** (Universal) and **Michael Collins** (Warner Bros.). Frank was a founder member of Fada Theatre Company in Donegal where he directed **Wild Harvest, The Tinkers' Wedding, Riders to the Sea** and **Translations** for An Grianán.

GINA MOXLEY NORA

Gina's previous Rough Magic appearances include **Mrs. Sweeney, The Way of the World, Digging for Fire** and **New Morning** (co-produced by The Bush Theatre, London). Other theatre credits include: **The Playboy of the Western World** and **Our Father** (Almeida, London); **Duck** (Out of Joint/Royal Court); **Iphigenia at Aulis** (Abbey); **Attaboy, Mr Synge** (Civic Theatre and tour); **Mistress of Silence** (Best Actress nomination, 1999 Irish Times/ESB Theatre Awards) and **The River** (Meridian). Film credits include **Saltwater, This is My Father, The Butcher Boy, The Sun, The Moon and the Stars** and **Snakes and Ladders**. Television credits include **The Ambassador, Family, Fair City, No Tears** and **Any Time Now**. Gina's playrighting credits include **Danti-Dan, Toupees and Snare Drums, Dog House, Tea Set, Marrying Dad** and **Swan's Cross**.

SINÉAD MURPHY RUBY

This is Sinéad's first appearance with Rough Magic. Other theatre credits include: **Romeo and Juliet** (Cork Opera House); **Blithe Spirit** (the Gate); **Alice in Wonderland** (the Civic); **Bimbo** (Common Currency); **Talbot's Box** (Bare Bodkin); **The Doomsday Cabaret** (Hiho Productions); **Scaredy-Cats** (Barnstorm); **Eclipsed** (Town Hall, Galway); **Spring** (Anam Productions); **Jack Straw** (Da Mob Productions); **Tension, Abbattoir Bags, The Good Sisters** and **Shakers** (3 Bags Full) and **Educating Rita** (Andrew's Lane). Film and television credits include: **The Marriage** (award winning short which she also produced); **I Could Read The Sky; Flick;** and **The Matchmaker**. Sinéad performs her own one-woman cabaret show, **An Evening with Cheryl Summers**, and she sings with the acapello trio **The Doomsdaisies**.

CATHY WHITE CLARA

Cathy's first appearance with Rough Magic was in **Shiver** (2002). Other theatre credits include: **Blackwater Angel, The Barbaric Comedies, As The Beast Sleeps, Tarry Flynn** and **The Trojan Women** (Abbey and Peacock); **Force of Change** and **The Weir** (Royal Court, London); **Stone and Ashes** (Dublin Theatre Festival); **Dancing at Lughnasa** (Lyric Theatre, Belfast) and seasons with the Royal Shakespeare Company, Royal National Theatre, Cheek By Jowl and Manchester's Royal Exchange. Film and television credits include **Murphy's Law, The Return, On Home Ground, The Cry, Perfect, Vicious Circle, Titanic Town, Saoirse, Night Train, The General, Snakes and Ladders, Nothing Personal, Grushko, The Big O** and **The Buddha of Suburbia**.

MARIE BREEN PRODUCTION MANAGER

Marie has previously worked with Rough Magic on **Olga, Shiver, Copenhagen, Dead Funny, Pentecost, The Whisperers** and **The School for Scandal**. Other recent work includes: **The Drunkard** (B*spoke); **Mermaids** (CoisCéim); Dublin Theatre Festival 2003 and 2002; the first International Dance Festival 2002; **The Book of Evidence** (Kilkenny Arts Festival/Fiach MacConghail); **My Brilliant Divorce** (Druid); **The Silver Tassie, The Flying Dutchman, Lady Macbeth of Mtsensk** and **Madama Butterfly** (Opera Ireland); **L'Altro Mondo** (Opera Machine); **Bread and Circus, Peeling Venus** and **The Salt Cycle** (Rex Levitates); **Macbeth, Romeo and Juliet** and **King Lear** (Second Age).

BREEGE BRENNAN PROPS BUYER

Breege has previously worked for Rough Magic as Administrator on **Midden**. Originally from Sligo, she has worked in professional theatre for 15 years. Other theatre credits include **Starlight Express** (West End, London) and productions with several Irish companies including The Gate, Fishamble and the Abbey. She has toured nationally and internationally with productions including **The Beckett Festival** (the Gate/Barbican and New Ambassadors, London) and **Pride and Prejudice** (the Gate/Spoleto Festival, Charleston, USA).

JOHN COMISKEY LIGHTING DESIGNER

John has previously worked with Rough Magic as Set and Lighting Designer on **Shiver** and **Copenhagen** (for which he won Best Designer in the 2002 Irish Times/ESB Irish Theatre Awards), and as Lighting Designer on **Three Days of Rain, Pentecost, The Way of the World, Love and a Bottle** and **The Country Wife.** Other lighting designs include productions for the Abbey, Druid, Daghdha, Siamsa Tire, Project, and the dance/jewellery installation, **Lifecycles,** at the Crafts Council. Recent credits include Set and Lighting Designer on **Mermaids** (CoisCéim) and he co-designed the set and lighting for **The Shape of Metal** (Abbey) with Alan Farquharson.

John co-devised and directed **The Well** at the Dublin Theatre Festival 2000 and Gavin Friday's **Ich Liebe Dich**, to the music of Kurt Weill, at the Dublin Theatre Festival 2001. John was Production Director with **Riverdance: The Show** for two years, and was Artistic Director of Operating Theatre (with Roger Doyle) from 1984-1989. During this period he also collaborated with James Coleman as Lighting Designer on **Ignotum per Ignotius**, at the Douglas Hyde Gallery, and as Lighting and Video Designer on the installation/performance **Guaire: an Allegory in Dunguaire**, Kinvara.

He directed **Hit and Run**, Ireland's first dance film, which won the main prizes at the Toronto Moving Pictures and New York Dance On Screen festivals. John has also directed and produced documentaries on the **Dingle Wrens' Day** and the **Berlin Years of Agnes Bernelle.** He was a director with RTÉ for 12 years, during which time he directed hundreds of television programmes and created the visual style of numerous TV series including **Nighthawks, The Blackbird and The Bell** and PopScene. In 1995, he directed the **Eurovision Song Contest.**

ALAN FARQUHARSON SET DESIGNER

This is Alan's first production with Rough Magic. Other theatre designs include: **West Side Story, A Life, Bugsy Malone** and **Rent** (Olympia); **Borstal Boy** and **Sinbad** (Gaiety) and **An Solas Dearg** (Peacock). He recently co-designed the set and lighting for **The Shape of Metal** (Abbey) with John Comiskey. He joined the RTÉ Design Department in 1978 where he designed for **The Late Late Show, Kenny Live, Prime Time,** RTÉ News presentations and various outside broadcasts. He has worked as Production Designer on many of RTÉ's major film productions including **Dear Sarah, Diary of a Madman, The Truth About Clare, Hello Stranger** and **The Treaty**. He was also responsible for the Production Design of the **Eurovision Song Contest** in 1993 and 1995 and **Gael Force** (Point Theatre). Since leaving RTÉ as Senior Production Designer in August 1996, he has been responsible for the design of **Night Train**

(Subotica Productions); **A Love Divided** (Parallel Films in association with RTÉ); **The Irish Tenors** (RDS/Waterfront, Belfast for Radius Television/PBS); **Relative Strangers** (Littlebird/Tatfilm); **A Secret Affair** (CBS/Adelson Entertainment/Metropolitan Films) and **The Nobel Peace Prize Concert** 1999 and 2000 (NRK Television).

Alan studied at the National College of Art & Design and now lectures in Production Design and Computer Aided Design at Dun Laoghaire Institute of Art, Design & Technology and has served on the council of The Institute of Designers in Ireland.

LAURA FORREST-HAY COMPOSER

This is Laura's first production with Rough Magic. Other theatre credits include: **Sharon's Grave** and **Sive** (Druid); **Iphigenia at Aulis** (Abbey) and **Famine** (rehearsed reading – Abbey); **Treehouses** and **Amazing Grace** (Peacock); **The Grapes of Wrath** and **Hard Times** (Storytellers); **The Carnival King** and **The Nun's Wood** (Fishamble); **Translations** (An Grianán); **The Dead School** (Macnas); **Riders to the Sea, Wild Harvest** and **April Bright** (Fada); **An Ideal Husband, The Crack** and **The Whip** (Galloglass); **Four Storeys** (Gúna Nua); **Anna Christie** (Focus); **Licking The Marmalade Spoon** (Baois); **The Playboy of The Western World** (Redgrave, England) and **Frankenstein's Mothers** (Foursight, England). Music composed for television includes: **Sir Gawain and the Green Knight** (BAFTA Best Animation 2002 – Moving Still/C4); **TV Dinners** (C4); **Farmleigh, Story of A House** (RTE) and **Rowlandson** (Moving Still). Music composed for film includes: **Bodyblow** (Schipa Films); **Filleann an Feall** (Flushfilms/TG4); **Countess Cathleen/The Yeats Trilogy** (produced by Patrick Bergin and Crimson Films) and **Bittersweet** (Journeyman Productions). As a professional musician, Laura was a member of **The Big Geraniums** and **Jack L's band**. She also acts and plays Irish traditional music professionally.

JUSTIN MURPHY STAGE MANAGER

This is Justin's first production with Rough Magic. He previously worked on **IL Giuramento** and **Sapho** (Wexford Festival Opera), **La Belle Helene** and **The Marriage of Figaro** (Castleward Opera) and **Our Country's Good** and **The Madras House** (BADA, London). He has also worked as a facilitator for Young Barecheek Drama School, Wexford and Bui Bolg Street Theatre.

EIMER NÍ MHAOLDOMHNAIGH COSTUME DESIGNER

This is Eimer's first production with Rough Magic. Other theatre costume design credits include: **Made in China** (Peacock); **Please Don't Make Me Feel So Happy** (Olympia); and **Translations** (Hands Turn). Eimer's numerous film and television costume design credits include: **In America; Proof; Timbuktu; The Most Fertile Man in Ireland; Rebel Heart; About Adam; The Ambassador; The Castle; Gold in the Streets** and most recently, **Omagh** for Channel 4.

PAULA TIERNEY STAGE DIRECTOR

Paula's previous productions with Rough Magic include **Olga, Shiver, Copenhagen, Pentecost, Northern Star, Danti Dan, Hidden Charges, The Dogs** and **Digging for Fire**. Paula is a graduate of UCC and has spent ten years as a stage manager/operator on productions for Fishamble, Second Age, Bickerstaffe, Barabbas, Galloglass, Calypso, Red Kettle, the Everyman, the Gate and the Peacock. She has toured nationally and internationally with Opera Theatre Company, including **Zaide** (Antwerp), **The Magic Flute, Cosi Fan Tutte, The Marriage of Figaro, La Vera Constanza** and **Amadigi** (Melbourne Festival/BAM, New York/Lisbon/Porto/Paris). She has been Stage Director for both the Covent Garden and Buxton opera festivals and in Dublin for Opera Ireland on **Die Fledermaus, La Traviata, Boris Godunov** and **Aïda**. Other recent productions include: **Macbeth** (Second Age); **The Quest of the Good People** (Pavilion); **Kvetch** (Kilkenny Arts Festival); **Mermaids** (CoisCéim) and **Wexford Festival Opera**.

ROUGH MAGIC PRODUCTIONS

2003
OLGA by Laura Ruohonen in a new version by
Linda McLean - IP

SHIVER by Declan Hughes - WP

2002
SCAN (international play-readings)
SEEDS new writing initiative, in association
with the Dublin Fringe Festival.

COPENHAGEN by Michael Frayn - IP

2001
MIDDEN by Morna Regan - WP
DEAD FUNNY by Terry Johnson - IP

PLAYS[4] (international play-readings)

2000
THREE DAYS OF RAIN
by Richard Greenberg - IP

PLAYS[4] (international play-readings)
PENTECOST by Stewart Parker - USP

1999
THE WHISPERERS Francis Sheridan's 'A Trip
to Bath' as completed by Elizabeth Kuti - WP

BOOMTOWN by Pom Boyd, Declan Hughes
and Arthur Riordan - WP

1998
THE SCHOOL FOR SCANDAL
by Richard Brinsley Sheridan

1997
HALLOWEEN NIGHT by Declan Hughes - WP

MRS. SWEENEY by Paula Meehan - WP

1996
PENTECOST by Stewart Parker

NORTHERN STAR by Stewart Parker

1995
DANTI-DAN by Gina Moxley - WP

PENTECOST by Stewart Parker

1994
LADY WINDERMERE'S FAN by Oscar Wilde
DOWN ONTO BLUE by Pom Boyd - WP

HIDDEN CHARGES by Arthur Riordan - WP

1993
NEW MORNING by Declan Hughes - WP

THE WAY OF THE WORLD by William Congreve

1992
DIGGING FOR FIRE by Declan Hughes - UKP
BAT THE FATHER RABBIT THE SON
by Donal O'Kelly
LOVE AND A BOTTLE by George Farquhar,
adapted by Declan Hughes

THE DOGS by Donal O'Kelly - WP
THE EMERGENCY SESSION
by Arthur Riordan - WP

1991

LOVE AND A BOTTLE by George Farquhar,
adapted by Declan Hughes - WP
LADY WINDERMERE'S FAN by Oscar Wilde

I CAN'T GET STARTED
by Declan Hughes - USP
DIGGING FOR FIRE by Declan Hughes - WP

1990

LADY WINDERMERE'S FAN by Oscar Wilde
I CAN'T GET STARTED
by Declan Hughes - WP

BAT THE FATHER RABBIT THE SON
by Donal O'Kelly

1989

BAT THE FATHER RABBIT THE SON
by Donal O'Kelly - UKP
A HANDFUL OF STARS by Billy Roche - IP

SPOKESONG by Stewart Parker
OUR COUNTRY'S GOOD
by Timberlake Wertenbaker - IP

1988

THE WHITE DEVIL by John Webster - IP
TOM AND VIV by Michael Hastings - IP
TEA AND SEX AND SHAKESPEARE
a new version by Thomas Kilroy

BAT THE FATHER RABBIT THE SON
by Donal O'Kelly - WP
SERIOUS MONEY by Caryl Churchill - IP

1987

NIGHTSHADE by Stewart Parker
ROAD by Jim Cartwright - IP
THE TEMPEST by Shakespeare
THE SILVER TASSIE by Sean O'Casey

A MUG'S GAME adaptation by the
company of Le Bourgeois Gentilhomme
and Everyman - IP

1986

MIDNITE AT THE STARLITE
by Michael Hastings
CAUCASIAN CHALK CIRCLE
by Bertolt Brecht
BETRAYAL by Harold Pinter - IP
**DOGG'S HAMLET, CAHOOT'S
MACBETH** by Tom Stoppard

DECADENCE by Steven Berkoff
AUNT DAN AND LEMON
by Wallace Shawn - IP
BLOODY POETRY by Howard Brenton
THE COUNTRY WIFE by William Wycherly
THE WOMAN IN WHITE adapted by Declan
Hughes from Wilkie Collins's novel - IP

1985

TOP GIRLS by Caryl Churchill
SEXUAL PERVERSITY IN CHICAGO
by David Mamet
VICTORY by Howard Barker - IP
NO END OF BLAME by Howard Barker - IP

THE ONLY JEALOUSY OF EMER by WB Yeats
MIDNITE AT THE STARLITE
by Michael Hastings - IP
CAUCASIAN CHALK CIRCLE
by Bertolt Brecht

1984

TALBOT'S BOX by Thomas Kilroy
FANSHEN by David Hare - IP
THE BIG HOUSE by Brendan Behan
THIRST by Myles na gCopaleen
DECADENCE by Steven Berkoff - IP

SEXUAL PERVERSITY IN CHICAGO
by David Mamet
TOP GIRLS by Caryl Churchill - IP
AMERICAN BUFFALO by David Mamet

WP = World première
IP = Irish première

UKP = UK première
USP = American première

FOR ROUGH MAGIC

ARTISTIC DIRECTOR **LYNNE PARKER**
EXECUTIVE PRODUCER **LOUGHLIN DEEGAN**
ADMINISTRATOR **ELIZABETH WHYTE**

BOARD OF DIRECTORS:

MARK MORTELL (CHAIR)
PAUL BRADY
MARIE BREEN
DARRAGH KELLY
JOHN McGOLDRICK
DERMOT McLAUGHLIN
PAULINE McLYNN
JOHN O'DONNELL

ADVISORY COUNCIL:

SIOBHÁN BOURKE
ANNE BYRNE
CATHERINE DONNELLY
DECLAN HUGHES
DARRAGH KELLY
PAULINE McLYNN
HÉLÈNE MONTAGUE
MARTIN MURPHY
ARTHUR RIORDAN
STANLEY TOWNSEND

ROUGH MAGIC THEATRE COMPANY

5/6 South Great Georges Street, Dublin 2, Ireland
T: + 353 1 6719278 **F:** + 353 1 6719301
E: info@rough-magic.com **W:** www.rough-magic.com
Registered number: 122753

Rough Magic gratefully acknowledges the support of the Arts
Council of Ireland, Dublin City Council and our Patrons.

ROUGH MAGIC PATRONS

Abhann Productions
Behaviour & Attitudes
Desmond Barry
Lorraine Brennan Management
Elma Carey
Catherine Cashman Santoro
Curtis Brown Group
Diageo Ireland
Catherine Donnelly
Marie Donnelly
Barry Dooley & S Lambe
Declan Doyle
John & Kaye Fanning
Philip & Nicola Flynn
Helen & Vincent Foley
Finbarr Fox
First Call Management
Brian Halford
The Terence & Mathilda Kennedy Charitable Trust
O J Kilkenny & Co
Julie Kay & Tom Fergus
Geoffrey & Jane Keating
Denis Looby
Conor & Louise Maguire
John Mahoney
Pat Mangan
R J McBratney
Denis McCullough
Eoin McCullough
David & Julie McMullan
Pat Moylan
Carmel Naughton
David Nolan
Theresa Nolan
Noel O'Brien
Dr Cormac Ó Cuilleanáin
O'Donnell Tuomey
John O'Donnell & Micheline Huggard
Dr Veronica O'Keane
George & Margaret Parker
Zita Reihill & John Gleeson
Lisa Richards Agency
David Soden
Sparrow Family
Paul Ward
Bill & Denise Whelan
Jonathan White
Whyte's Irish Art Auctioneers & Valuers
....and those who prefer to remain anonymous

WORDS OF ADVICE FOR YOUNG PEOPLE

Ioanna Anderson

'The first signs of a mutual attraction will induce
even the inconsolable to live in the present.'

Cyril Connolly, *The Unquiet Grave*

For A.J. and for the Greenlights
and in memory of Ruby Collins

2

Characters

NORA GOLDEN, *thirty-eight, runs unsuccessful B&B in a remote part of Leitrim*

CLARA GOLDEN, *thirty-five, her sister, a successful TV actress*

DANNY BRENNAN, *Nora's husband*

ROB KELLY, *Nora's oldest and best friend, a journalist*

JACK McBURNEY, *the local undertaker*

RUBY, *Jack's wife*

ACT ONE

Scene One

The stage is dark. Onstage is JACK, *driving in a car.* RUBY *is with him, sitting beside or behind him. During the play,* RUBY *will always be onstage when* JACK *is, although none of the other characters can see or hear her.* JACK *doesn't look at her directly, except where this is specified in the stage directions, although he can hear her.*

A voice in the dark.

RUBY. Why is it so dark? (*Pause.*) Jack?

> JACK *says nothing. Lights a cigarette.*

Put your lights on. What are you doing? Put your lights on!

> JACK *puts his headlights on.* JACK *and* RUBY *are both clearly visible now.*

JACK. There's nothing on the road. There's no-one.

RUBY. There's a light on over the pub, still.

JACK. She never turns that off.

RUBY. Slow down.

JACK. My father always said, be careful who you travel in a car with, because –

RUBY. Slow down –

JACK. – something about the way people talk to each other, travelling in a car, you'd be liable to tell a person anything they wanted to know.

RUBY. Anything?

JACK. He wasn't much of a talker at the best of times.

RUBY. It's late. Go home.

JACK. We still advertise a 24-hour service. Though Pete always says, 'Beyond the fuckin' call. If they're dead it can wait till office hours. Put some pennies on their eyes and call us in the morning.'

We don't get that many calls.

RUBY. It's a small town. You can nearly drive past it in the dark and not see it's a town.

JACK. The town's changing. My father knew every one of the people he buried.

RUBY. And his father before him. I know this one.

JACK. I think he loved his job.

RUBY. Your father didn't use words like 'love'.

JACK. I read somewhere, some politician, I can't remember who, said you could measure a people's respect for the laws of the land by the way they cared for their dead. My father always went out when people called. Day or night.

At his funeral, it seemed like the whole town lined up to shake my hand. They remembered he came out to them in the night when the worst happened. He kept their secrets. You want to know what goes on in a place like this, ask the doctor, the priest and the undertaker.

RUBY. They won't tell you, but they know.

JACK. Marie down at the mortuary in Sligo, when I showed up tonight she said: 'Can't this wait till the morning?' But she's always pleased to see someone. She's been doing that job twenty years, loading things people don't want to see in and out of vans in the middle of the night. She said, 'This's an odd one, now. I heard about him. You won't be needing the trolley, sure.'

RUBY. Been dead a long time.

JACK. Five years. It's taken them three weeks to identify what's left of Harry Golden. I signed for him and Marie handed me over this small container, just about the size of a shoebox, sealed with tape.

RUBY. What's the rush?

JACK. I'm not rushing for him.

RUBY. That house on the corner with the pink gates. I always liked that house.

JACK. When I was sixteen, the man who owned that house killed himself with a shotgun. Bank holiday weekend, the rest of the family was in Dublin for a wedding. Me and my dad spent the whole weekend repainting his living room before the family came home and saw the mess.

RUBY. They said it was an accident but everybody knew.

JACK. I had to clean the floor. So much blood had seeped into the wood, I sanded it down twice but you could see the stain. His family still live in that house.

RUBY. What way are you going?

JACK. This is the way I always go.

RUBY. You could take the road up by the post office.

JACK. This road is fine.

RUBY. It's quicker if you go by the post office.

JACK. Remember that row of cottages next to the Murphys' place? Young couple moved there from the city, fixed them up.

RUBY. Why don't you just go by the post office?

JACK. They did all the work on the house themselves. It's beautiful inside. Husband goes out to walk the dog one evening, falls down unconscious, dies. Heart attack. He was a healthy man in his thirties. His wife never spent another night in that house. She told me it was like staring into his open coffin. The dead need to be buried, she said.

RUBY. Sooner or later.

JACK *doesn't respond. A pause.*

Turn right by the post office.

JACK. They're demolishing that old bungalow –

RUBY. Turn right by the post office.

JACK. That bungalow, over behind the field, there – remember? – with the broken steps –

RUBY. Turn right.

JACK. Belonged to a little old lady living on her own, neighbours hadn't seen her for a while, looked through the letter box, smelled something bad, called the Guards.

RUBY. Turn right –

JACK. She was on the bed, looked like she hadn't been able to get up for a while. Bed was soaked in her piss and shit, we had to haul the mattress out and burn it.

RUBY. Turn right –

JACK. Relatives standing in the living room bickering about money and furniture while we carried her out. She had five children living locally and she died all alone in a pile of her own shit.

It is a very small town.

Blackout.

Scene Two

We are in the garden of the Goldens' large, ramshackle house in Co. Leitrim. A gnome garden, Harry Golden's bizarre collection, is laid out over the lawns as far as the eye can see. Hundreds of gnomes. There's a signpost saying B&B with an arrow pointing upstage – towards the house. There is a table and some garden chairs on the lawn. There's an umbrella leaning against the table. NORA comes onstage carrying cups and sandwiches. She lays them on the table. DANNY comes in after her, stands behind her and gathers up her hair off her neck, and turns her round. ROB enters, NORA turns to greet him, DANNY is still holding her hair at the back of her neck as they start speaking.

DANNY. Rob!

ROB. Danny?

DANNY. Rob!

ROB (DANNY *has taken* ROB*'s hand and is shaking it vigorously.*) Danny.

NORA. Rob.

ROB. Are we just going to do this for a while?

DANNY. Howareyeh!

ROB. It's hard to say.

DANNY. Surprised to see me, huh?

ROB. Surprised – isn't the word.

DANNY. Long time!

ROB. Feels like yesterday.

DANNY. Four years, is it?

ROB. Five.

DANNY. Go 'way!

ROB. Yep. Feels shorter. Come here, gorgeous. (*Pulls* NORA *into a long hug, disengaging her from* DANNY.) Hello again.

NORA. Hello. I thought you were lost.

ROB. I was lost. Drove down every unmarked single-track dirt road in the back arse of nowhere in the rain looking for this colourful little pothole you call home. How did I ever find this place before?

NORA. You didn't. Last time you misread the map and ended up in Donegal.

ROB. Maps, I have discovered, are largely useless in this, the Country Without Signposts. I'm not clear even now are we technically in Sligo, in Leitrim or in the merry fucking land of Oz.

NORA. I wrote out the directions for you.

ROB. So you did. Ten pages WITH DIAGRAMS, the only thing makes any sense is, if you've hit Bundoran you've gone too far.

DANNY. Beautiful Bundoran.

ROB. Bundoran is not beautiful.

NORA. It's a song.

ROB. Remain calm, I tell myself, roll down the window, ask the next village idiot for directions. I find a little man wearing an apron cleaning windows in a caravan park, I understand about one word in seven and I fail to catch the meaning of the one word. I consult the manual. Your handwriting, angel, is like the Book of Kells. Page *seven* starts, 'Look out for the pub with the goat.'

DANNY. Micky Hanlon's goat. At the crossroads?

ROB. Indeed. Tourist goat. Tied up outside the hotel trying to look authentic, 'I got the gig'. Ah, the countryside is lovely, certainly. I just can't see why anyone would consider living here.

NORA. Thank you for coming.

ROB. It was an adventure. So. What are we doing out here?

NORA. Having a drink. And then, having another drink. (*She struggles to open the bottle of wine,* DANNY *takes it from her and opens it with a flourish, pours wine.*)

ROB. Are we hiding?

DANNY. Americans.

ROB. Where?

NORA. Six Americans, four nights B&B, they booked it months ago. Said they're from some Harry and Margaret Golden Appreciation Society. They showed up yesterday wearing horrible little badges saying 'Colin the Rabbit says Howdy'. They took photographs of me, the gnomes, the shed, they found a mug in the kitchen that says 'Harry' on it and they took a photo of that too. They've brought this poster-sized copy of their family tree and they keep trying to explain to me how they are in fact descended from an O'Neill although their name is Grotowski. If they ask me about the Famine I'm going to have to stab them in the throat with a fork.

ROB. Some little guy in a woolly hat intercepted me in the drive and told me you were out here.

NORA. Barry, my new friend. He fixes roofs. I met him in the butchers. He said: 'You have pigeons in your roof.' This turned out not to be a quaint local greeting. I have actual pigeons in my roof.

ROB. Is that bad?

NORA. He turned up this morning to give me an estimate with a vanful of other small men in woolly hats who kept breaking bits of the roof off with their bare hands and laughing. They've been here all day.

DANNY (*raising glass, the others follow*). *Sláinte.*

They drink.

So, what're you up to these days?

ROB. Same old, same old.

NORA. He's writing a novel.

DANNY. Weren't you – ?

ROB. Same novel.

DANNY. You're looking well anyway.

ROB. You're looking – expensive.

DANNY. I do OK.

ROB. Nice shoes.

DANNY. I came down when I heard, of course. About Harry.

ROB. Of course.

DANNY. Help Nora, y'know?

ROB (*pouring cup of tea, manages to pour some over* DANNY*'s hand while replacing the teapot*). I'm sorry. Did it – ?

DANNY. Not at all.

ROB (*looking around, grabs a cloth from a pile on top of the heaped cardboard boxes, to clean up the spill*). What's all this?

NORA. Amongst other things, a horrible portrait of mum and dad from the seventies, all the colours are too bright and they're smiling in this weird way makes them look like they have too many teeth. The Americans want to buy it. They offered me ten thousand dollars for the garden shed.

ROB (*rooting amongst pile of boxes, brings out a book and starts looking through it*). Aaah. '*Colin the Rabbit. By Harry and Margaret Golden.*' The lovely world of Colin the Rabbit and all his anthropomorphic little woodland friends skipping about having adventures.

DANNY. Yeah. And they were all home in time for tea.

ROB. They were good. I forgot how good they were.

NORA. The Americans wanted to know was Colin based on a real rabbit. That we knew personally.

ROB (*rummaging further, reading out titles*). '*Colin and the New Neighbours.*' '*Colin Goes to School.*' '*Colin Travels Further than Usual.*' I love that one. Did you know you have three tabloid photographers camped in your hedge?

DANNY. Four.

ROB. I don't suppose they're here to write up Harry's funeral arrangements.

NORA. They're waiting for Clara.

ROB. Fuckin' paparazzi. D'you want me to go and break someone's camera?

NORA. The Guards are keeping an eye on them. Apparently I can't have them removed until they start actually trespassing. I did have to ask one of them to move his car because it was blocking the laneway and the hearse can't get through.

DANNY. D'you read this morning's paper?

ROB. I'm trying to cut down.

DANNY (*finds newspaper, unfolds it and shows it to them*). Page seven, the big story.

ROB (*reads*). 'Is this the end of the affair?'

DANNY. (*reads*). 'With just weeks to go before their lavish society wedding . . . '

ROB. What wedding?

DANNY. ' . . . is it all over for the glamorous actress and her millionaire prince? These pictures were taken outside an exclusive London nightclub . . . ' Turn to page 18, big colour spread, photos of the bride-to-be falling out of a nightclub with unidentified escort. Big muscles.

ROB (*takes paper from* DANNY, *reads*). 'TV star Clara Golden, 28, refused to comment today as she left her luxury penthouse apartment, alone . . . ' She's not 28.

DANNY. Not a word to Nora about any of it.

ROB. And he's not a prince.

NORA *gets out a cigarette,* DANNY *lights it for her.*

DANNY. Her own sister.

ROB. Are there any more sandwiches?

NORA (*starts to get up*). Hundreds.

DANNY (*prevents* NORA *getting up, gets up himself*). My pleasure.

DANNY *exits.*

ROB. What wedding?

NORA. Your guess is as good as mine.

ROB. Is Danny living here?

NORA *says nothing, smokes.* ROB *relights her cigarette, which has gone out.*

Nora – ?

NORA. *Rob.* I'm tired, I'm premenstrual, my house is falling to bits, and now I have to improvise a cold buffet for a hundred locals who want to pay their respects and check out the scandal. You are the first person I've been pleased to see all day.

ROB. Why are you responsible for all the arrangements? Why is Clara not here?

NORA. She's on her way. I just didn't expect this many people. The notice in the paper said no letters or flowers to the house and only family and close friends at the service. I'm not – prepared. And the house is falling to bits.

ROB. Why is the house falling to bits?

NORA. I don't know. There are mice in the floorboards and frogs in the drain. The shutters are coming off their hinges and none of the doors close properly. Last week I painted all the kitchen cupboards and yesterday I found mould growing on the fresh paint.

ROB. Nora, my darlin'. I love you and you cook a spectacular breakfast but I have to tell you this B&B enterprise is stone fucking mad. I drove in through the town, there are four derelict houses on the main street, the only place I could get a cup of coffee was this greasy shed with the blinds down and a cardboard sign in the window saying 'COME IN! WE'RE OPEN!!' I saw half a dozen women on the street with thinning hair. The billboard over the post office has one huge picture of a cow and underneath it says 'THE ORIGINAL CELTIC TIGER'.

NORA. The town's a bit – depressed –

ROB. It's lying in bed in a foetal position with it's face turned to the wall.

NORA *does not respond.*

This town can support maybe one conveniently located
B&B and this is not it.

NORA. I know.

ROB. What's going on? How long has Danny been back here?
(*Silence from* NORA.) OK. OK. I won't say anything.
I won't say a word. You want to hunker down here in the
Valley of the Squinting Windows and make jam and babies
with that buffoon, I won't try and talk you out of it. Unless
you want me to. Nora? (NORA *visibly upset.*) Nora.

CLARA *enters before* NORA *can respond to this. She is
carrying some folders and bits of paper and looks more
expensive and confident than* NORA.

CLARA. Nora.

ROB. Gang's all here.

NORA. I was expecting you later. Did you get the earlier
flight?

CLARA (*hugs* NORA). How are you Rob? How's the novel?

ROB. I read a book once about a woman who thought she
wanted to write a novel but it eventually transpired she was
entirely mistaken and her true vocation was running a bagel
shop. (*Pause.*) Ah, y'know, Mondays always have this effect
on me.

CLARA. It's Wednesday, Robert.

ROB. You look well. Clara.

CLARA. I made a list.

ROB (*picking up one of her bits of paper and reading*).
'BAND HIRE: Frankly the Best – Call Vincent.'

CLARA (*removing this paper from* ROB). Wrong list.

ROB. They sing Frank, I take it.

NORA. And a bit of Elvis when the mood is upon them.
I quote.

ROB. Still marrying whatsisname then? (*Produces the newspaper.*)

CLARA (*glances at it, clearly has seen it before*). Is that your way of saying congratulations?

ROB. No.

CLARA. I saw Danny up at the house.

ROB. How'd he look to you?

CLARA. Same.

ROB. Like he's about to ask you to lend him money.

NORA. He's here to help.

ROB. Define help.

CLARA. He said to tell you the Americans need more towels and they want to know when it's going to stop raining.

ROB. Is it raining?

NORA. I told them it was a fine mist.

CLARA. What's Danny doing here?

ROB. Making sandwiches.

CLARA. When I saw him he was showing the Americans around the gnome garden and explaining how he's found God.

ROB. Everybody loves a reformed sinner.

CLARA. Is he reformed?

ROB. Ask Nora.

Pause.

CLARA. The Yanks love him. '*So Irish!*'

ROB. That's a good thing, right?

NORA. They're from Texas.

ROB. Maybe they could take him home, have him stuffed and mounted.

NORA. I'll be back shortly. Talk pleasantly amongst yourselves.

NORA exits. A brief silence.

CLARA. How've you been?

ROB. All right, thank you.

CLARA. Me too.

ROB. I know. I see you on TV.

CLARA. You watch the show?

ROB. It's gripping. I'm waiting to see when will your top fall off again.

CLARA. It's not all like that.

ROB. It's great. *Charlie's Angels* for the new millennium. Three strong liberated women with college educations and great tits. They wear leather. They fight crime. They get wet a lot. My boss loves it. He's thinks you're a lovely girl but you could stand to eat a few more sandwiches. (*Pause.*) I'm sorry about Harry.

CLARA. It's old news.

Pause. CLARA fiddles with a tape recorder, tries to play the tape in it. It is completely distorted. She stops the tape.

ROB. Wait.

CLARA. What?

ROB. Try it again.

CLARA tries the tape again. They listen.

Again.

CLARA stops, rewinds, presses play again.

Sounds like Harry.

They listen again. The first bit comes clear: 'Colin and the Big Fish, *by Harry and Margaret Golden, read by Harry Golden –' before it distorts again. It's hopelessly damaged. CLARA turns it off, quite abruptly.*

CLARA (*hands* ROB *a pamphlet*). Take a look at this.

ROB. (*reads*). 'SPIRITUALITY: TAKING A BREAK. Even Jesus needed a break from his disciples!' What is this?

CLARA (*points to the bottom of the pamphlet*). The Congregation of the Blessed Something Retreat Fund. Keep reading.

ROB. 'Even with all the changes and developments we see in our world, there are some things that never change. We all need peace and rest and quiet but sometimes we can't find them in today's busy, stressful . . . ' – OK, why am I reading this?

CLARA (*reads*). 'Jesus said to his disciples: "You must come away to a lonely place all by yourselves and rest for a while." Today, he might have said: "You poor things! You are wrecked from overwork!! Take a break."'

ROB. Did Danny write this?

CLARA. Not exactly.

ROB. I thought I recognised his promiscuous use of the exclamation mark.

CLARA. It's some bloke Danny met *in church*. David. Sorry, *Brother* David. He's 'really spiritual.' He spent *ten years teaching in India*. I asked Danny what he taught. Danny couldn't remember but thinks it might have been English As A Foreign Language. He handed me one of these when I walked in the door.

ROB. So?

CLARA. What do you think?

ROB. About what?

CLARA *doesn't reply to this*

Well, I think it's very nice Danny has a new friend in Jesus.

CLARA. You think Daniel is a buffoon. Fine. But even a buffoon can cause difficulties for an intelligent person. He tormented Nora for seven long years. He's a blight.

ROB. It's getting pretty biblical around here all of a sudden. One blight after another. I'm just waiting for the locusts to show up.

CLARA. It's not funny.

ROB. Did I say it was funny?

CLARA. Did you know he was back here?

ROB. No.

CLARA. Well –

ROB. Well?

CLARA. Well, what are we going to do about it?

ROB. What did you have in mind?

CLARA. You first.

ROB. I thought I could maybe just sit here quietly and wring my hands and hope for the best while maintaining a position of uncomfortable neutrality, in the inglorious tradition of my country.

CLARA. Danny Brennan. Fundraising for God. What's wrong with this picture?

ROB. Maybe he's anxious about the state of his immortal soul. Now that he's discovered he has one, and all.

CLARA. He's probably in there right now trying to persuade Nora to turn this place into some kind of – spiritual health farm with the Blessed Brother Thing and his disciples.

ROB. You're worried about the *house*?

CLARA. This is my childhood home.

ROB. Are you intending to *live* here?

CLARA. Maybe.

ROB. You think you have no privacy *now*. One main street and a petrol station, everyone knows who everyone is and *where* they are. A strange car parks outside your house and five minutes later they're all speculating about it in the butchers.

Ask Nora. It's not all lovely walks and picking mushrooms and tea on the lawn.

CLARA. Nora loves it here.

ROB. She'll snap out of it.

CLARA. You don't know anything about this place. You know about living in cities and not being connected to anything and fucking people you never see again.

ROB *shrugs. Pause.*

I'm worried about Nora.

ROB. Nora and Danny are grown-ups.

CLARA. There's no such thing as grown-ups. There's just men, and women.

ROB. And children.

Silence.

What do you want me to do?

CLARA. You could go and punch Danny.

ROB. I punched him five years ago. He punched me back.

CLARA. I thought we'd seen the last of him. I thought he'd been –

ROB. Banished? Exorcised?

CLARA. I turn my back for five minutes and here he is again. Feet under the table, making himself at home. It's like one of those fairy stories, with the bad fairy.

ROB. If you remember, in the story the bad fairy always has to be invited in.

NORA *re-enters, with second bottle of wine.*

NORA. It's stopped raining. The Yanks have borrowed my sensible footwear and gone out to find some scenery to take photographs of before dinner. I told them there was lots of it around, they couldn't miss it.

CLARA. Why are there men crawling around on the roof?

NORA. I thought it would be a nice touch. (*Pause.*) The roof is broken and the nice men are fixing it.

CLARA. What's wrong with the roof?

ROB. Pigeons. (*Offers cigarettes round. NORA takes one, CLARA doesn't.*)

CLARA. I gave up.

ROB. When?

CLARA. Monday. (*He lights her one and passes it to her. She takes it.*) So. What next? Where are the – remains?

NORA. The local Funeral Directors. McBurneys. They did mum's funeral. D'you remember? Old Mr McBurney and Young Mr McBurney.

ROB. Cute.

CLARA. No.

NORA. Old Mr McBurney's dead now. It's Young Mr McBurney who runs the business.

CLARA. Whatever.

NORA. He seems like a nice man.

ROB. Nora, you think everyone is nice.

NORA. He's coming today to talk to us about the funeral. And we need to talk to Dad's lawyer about the will.

CLARA. Great. (ROB *is rummaging through his pockets for more cigarettes, takes out various stray items, including a small Dictaphone. CLARA notices this.*) Are you *working*?

ROB. Not this minute.

CLARA. I thought you gave up journalism.

ROB. Not unless I want to give up eating.

NORA. What're you working on?

ROB. TV series. State of the nation's spiritual health. I've been interviewing a group of old people. Well, I ask them questions, they talk. Sometimes they answer the question.

NORA. And what are you asking them?

ROB. All the big Sunday night questions: birth, death, love, faith. If there is no God, what's replaced him? What consoling information stands between you and the meaningless absurdity of life. All we can know definitely is that we die.

NORA. Oh, boy.

CLARA. Keeping it light and sparkling, of course.

ROB. The whole human experience in five parts. We start at the end and work backwards.

NORA. Who are you interviewing?

ROB. Al, Ian, Ted and Dorothy.

NORA. Are they famous? Did they write a book?

ROB. They live in the same nursing home.

CLARA. Which qualifies them to dispense their theories on the meaning of life, apparently.

ROB. Why not? They're old. They're not senile. They're the same as they always were. They just got old and so will you. If you're lucky.

CLARA. Sounds like a real ratings winner.

ROB. Maybe. Find out how it all looks when you're coming up to the finishing line.

CLARA. And how does it look?

ROB. Tune in next Sunday.

CLARA. Birth and death I understand. It's the bit in between gives me trouble.

ROB. Ah, that's in Part Two. In Part Two I interview a professor who wrote a book about it. He talked a lot about *life choices*. Like marriage, for example. What do people get married for anymore? We discussed the changing role and status of marriage in the twenty-first century. He was very optimistic.

NORA. I read somewhere that more people are getting married now. It's back in fashion or something.

CLARA. I read that too. It was in *Marie Claire,* right after an article on people who give their pets plastic surgery.

ROB. Statistics show that more people marry during, before and after wars, famine, pestilence and natural disasters. It's an anxious time.

NORA. I wonder is that true. Is that why people get married?

ROB. You're asking the wrong man. (*To* CLARA.) Why are you getting married?

CLARA. Why not?

ROB. Now Harry and Margaret, there was the exemplary traditional happy marriage.

CLARA. Oh no. Rake up some cute anecdotal evidence from your own family.

ROB. Not one successful marriage in the whole family tree as far as anyone can remember. My mother left home when I was seven. After that every time my father left the house he put a note on the kitchen table for her: '*Gone out on important business. Back soon. Please wait.*' Eventually he just – stopped leaving the house.

CLARA. Did she come back?

ROB. No. (*Pause.*)

NORA. I thought you knew that story.

CLARA. No.

NORA. Look. I know this isn't exactly a fun social occasion but I haven't seen either of you for ages. I was really looking forward to it. (*To* ROB.) I thought you were bringing Annie down.

ROB. I thought I was too. Waited for her for three quarters of an hour in some pub full of beautiful flawless people under 25. I was talking to this nice girl behind the bar who said I reminded her of her little brother. She looked about 20.

I asked how old her little brother was. She said, she didn't have a little brother, but she imagined if she did have one, he'd be like me. What does that mean?

CLARA. It means she doesn't want to sleep with you.

NORA (*her phone rings, she looks at caller display, and answers it*). Danny? What? . . . I can't hear you . . . hang on, I'll see if I can get a better signal . . . (*Exits.*)

CLARA. Who's Annie?

ROB. Nice, cheerful Australian. She's doing an MA in Archaeology. She's 22, she speaks five European languages and she likes to walk round the house naked.

CLARA. What the hell are you doing with a 22-year-old?

ROB. She looks very nice walking around the house naked.

CLARA. She sounds perfect. Nubile, uncomplicated. Temporary.

ROB. I don't remember saying she was temporary.

NORA *re-enters.*

NORA. The catering van's got stuck in some mud at the end of the driveway. I have to call Brendan next door and ask him to dig them out with the tractor. Could one of you ask Danny to bring down some tea and biscuits for the McBurneys? (*Exits.*)

CLARA. Catering van? For chrissakes. What's going on here?

ROB. Nora's throwing a party.

CLARA. I thought we'd agreed. A small quiet service. Family and close friends.

ROB. Maybe you agreed. Nora's been down here on her own, running around trying to supervise a respectable send-off while you show up at the last minute and eat sandwiches.

CLARA. I came as soon as I could. Harry disappeared five years ago. We knew he was dead. We knew. We went through all this then. *Now* they find – I don't want to think about what they found. I don't want to be asked questions about it. I don't need some *do* with flowers and wine and people chatting on the lawn with plates of food in their hand and me and Nora sitting like a fucking cherry on top of it.

ROB. What does Nora need?

CLARA. Evidently some kind of love-in, where we all cry and hug each other and tell stories and *heal* and *grow*. I'd rather be beaten to death with my own arm.

ROB. That can be arranged.

CLARA. My parents wanted to donate their bodies to medical science. They signed papers. Harry showed me. At the bottom of the form it asked, 'Do you want relatives/next of kin informed about any memorial services?' and he'd ticked 'NO'. By the time my mother died, her body was so destroyed by the illness we cremated her anyway. And now Harry. All we've got is a hand and some bones.

ROB. My dad was cremated. He signed up for one of those pre-death packages, where it's all ordered and paid for in advance. He didn't want to be a bother. He was just – cleared away.

CLARA. Harry is not being cleared away. Even if we wanted to, even if we wanted to, we can't forget. He's all over this house, this garden, he's Nora's nose, my feet and the way I say certain words. He's why I play everything to win, he's why I can lay carpet and order dinner in French. He's why Nora and I know the lyrics of every Frank Sinatra song recorded before 1960. I don't need to stand beside a pile of earth and a fancy coffin to remind me of Harry.

ROB. What does Nora need?

CLARA. She needs to look around. The dead are bloody everywhere. You can't move in this place without tripping over them. But they're dead and I'm alive and I don't need to be made to stare *that* in the face again with a bunch of strangers who came to watch the show.

ROB. Couple of months after my dad died, the Funeral Home sent me out a letter, saying they had his ashes. 'Could I please come and pick them up within thirty days or incur a monthly

storage charge.' I went, the guy behind the desk took me
into a shed behind the main building. Just a shed, piled high
with boxes of ashes. He told me people kept failing to
collect the ashes and they were going to have to rent more
storage space. They couldn't throw the ashes away because
sometimes the relatives showed up, years later, even,
wanting – well, call it what you like. He said, people don't
know what to do any more. There's no etiquette. There's no
rules. He said they missed God.

CLARA. The dead are finished. It would be very pretty to
believe in something else but I can't. I think it's a gyp.

ROB. Maybe.

CLARA. You believe in something else? Really?

ROB. I'll believe in whatever helps.

CLARA. Oh, sure, maybe I should truck on down to the local
church, listen to the priest pump the crowd full of beautiful,
phoney fellow feeling that lasts all the way to the car park.
Why not? Borrow some more pamphlets from Danny's new
friend, see if I can't paddle my way to the afterlife in my
own home-made consoling bullshit. Oh Jesus. Danny.
(*Brings out a mobile phone, dials* DANNY*'s number.*)
Danny? It's Clara. Nora says would you bring down some
tea and biscuits for the Funeral People. And milk and sugar.
Milk and sugar. For the tea.

I can't bear another funeral like my mother's. I just don't
think I can bear it. I didn't want it, Harry didn't want it,
Mum didn't want it, but there we were, lined up outside the
church, shaking everyone's hand. All those fucking people,
rows and rows of hats and shoulders and all those words
that didn't mean shit to me. And I couldn't take my eyes off
the coffin, the thought of my mother, inside, her body. I
couldn't forget what we were putting in the ground. I
couldn't think about the lid closing on her and I couldn't
think about anything else and it doesn't matter how you
dress it up. Nora can sing songs and plant trees and visit the
piece of earth we put them in, and fucking *cherish*
everything, but they're dead and gone and it doesn't help

me, it doesn't help me. I keep thinking, I want to go home, which is so – (stupid) because – I am home. I am home. (*Phone rings again, interrupting her. She answers it, it's* DANNY *again.*) I don't know how many, bring a few cups. A few. Some. Two. A pot of tea. (*Rings off.*) For chrissakes. He does it on purpose to annoy me. (*Stomps off to get the tea herself.*)

ROB *tries the tape again. This time the next few words come clearly: '. . . read by Harry Golden . . . Once upon a time, a very long time ago, before it started to rain, Colin woke up from a deep deep sleep – ' then distorts again.* ROB *turns it off.*

ROB. Well, H, it's going great so far. Maybe this is a dream. Maybe I'm going to wake up soon. You're going to say, if that had been a dream, I definitely would've had the last word. Of course, I don't dream about Clara.

NORA *comes in behind him.*

NORA. Of course.

ROB. Actually I keep dreaming that my bath is full of oversized keyrings. What do you think that means?

NORA. Perhaps it means you should finish your novel.

ROB. Or, you know, maybe it just means I need a new keyring.

NORA. Don't be angry with me.

ROB. Not with you.

NORA. He just turned up. I didn't know what to do.

ROB. Call the police?

NORA. Danny loved Harry, you know. Harry was like a father to him.

ROB. Yeah, he did that a lot, old Harry.

NORA. Danny was my first love. They say you never really get over your first love.

ROB. They say a lot of things.

NORA. He just – took up so much space, for so long. He got so big, I couldn't imagine – I couldn't see – past him.

ROB. He's not so big.

NORA. Not to you.

ROB. Nora. Look around. It's not Danny. It was never really Danny, blocking your light.

CLARA *enters, carrying a tray full of teacups, teapot, milk, etc.* NORA *comes after, takes it from her and starts organising tea.*

CLARA. Coming up: tea on the lawn, followed by more tea. Meeting with the Funeral Directors at which tea will be taken. After which, someone will almost certainly go and make tea. Any questions?

ROB (*looking around*). I have a question. Yeah. Why *gnomes*?

NORA. Did Danny not bring tea down?

CLARA. He was on the phone and then he went off somewhere.

NORA. Went where, for God's sake?

CLARA. Don't fuss about it.

NORA. I'm not.

CLARA. You are fussing. It's not important.

NORA. I'll be back in a minute. (*Exits.*)

CLARA. For chrissakes.

ROB. You might choose your words more carefully.

CLARA. Fussing exactly describes what she was doing.

ROB. You just got here. You don't know what she's doing.

ROB *exits after* NORA.

DANNY *enters, carrying a large tray loaded with tea, cups, saucers, milk, etc.*

DANNY. Tea for anyone?

Blackout.

ACT TWO

Scene One

JACK, *sitting, then pacing, checking watch, smoking, straightening his suit, etc. while waiting to go in to the Goldens' house.* RUBY *is with him, as before.*

JACK. First time I met you. Christmas. Somebody's party. I can't remember whose. Maybe I didn't know.

RUBY. I was sitting on the stairs.

JACK. You were sitting on the stairs. I can't remember what you were wearing or what way your hair was and I wouldn't have been able to tell anyone the colour of your eyes, if they'd asked me. I never saw you before that night.

RUBY. I saw you.

JACK. I walked up to you and I said –

RUBY. You said, 'Why did I never see you before?' I said I was up visiting my cousin.

JACK. Fidelma.

RUBY. Fiona.

JACK. You'd sliced your hand on the broken neck of a beer bottle someone left on the ground. I lent you a handkerchief to put round it and the handkerchief turned red. You said you'd wash it and send it back to me.

RUBY. You said you'd call me and tell me where to send it. You were very definite. You'd call and we'd meet.

JACK. By then – We'd talked a long time by then. I remembered it a long time afterwards.

RUBY. We drank most of a bottle of whisky someone had abandoned outside one of the bedrooms. And you spoke very beautifully about your family, about why you didn't go to college, about why my eyes were extraordinary, and the death of your first dog, aged twelve.

JACK. You wrote your number on a piece of paper I put in my wallet and then you wrote it on the back of my hand. I walked you home, which was three miles. We sat on your aunt's garage wall until people started coming out of their houses for mass.

RUBY. When you got up to leave, I noticed you'd been holding my hand.

JACK. I went to bed and slept like – like something heavy had been lifted from me, and when I woke up it was dark.

RUBY. The next day a helpful friend of yours let me know you were engaged to someone called Bernie. You hadn't mentioned it.

JACK. I woke up and I went straight to your aunt's house. I didn't know how long you were staying, if you'd gone home already –

RUBY. I answered the door. You said 'Yes, I was engaged to someone named Bernie. Until recently. Until yesterday, if that's interesting.' I said it was very interesting.

JACK. I've told that story so many times.

You know that game, that you play at kids' parties. I don't know if they still play it. It's a memory game. There's a bunch of objects on a tray and the tray's covered with a cloth. Everyone has a bit of paper and a pencil and the cloth's lifted off the tray for, I don't know, ten, twenty, thirty seconds. And you look at all the things on the tray and you try and remember as many of them as you can before the cloth comes back down over them. And then you write down what you remember. I was terrible at that game. I'd be staring at the things so hard trying to remember and as soon as they disappeared I'd forget it all, just from trying so hard to remember.

Now – I can't forget anything now.

Pause. He turns around to find RUBY *but she's gone.*

If you knew – if you knew the last times were the last times, I think it would be –

I think it would probably be unbearable.

Throws down cigarette and stubs it out. Walks offstage.

Blackout.

Scene Two

Back on the lawn with the gnomes, ROB *is drinking the tea on the tray and he has a book on his knee which he is reading but puts face down on the table when* CLARA *enters, wet haired, rubbing her head with a towel.*

CLARA. I think it's raining.

ROB. You always think it's raining. (*Nevertheless, he produces an umbrella from his side of the table, with theatrical flourish, sets it up so* CLARA *is underneath it.*)

CLARA. The light's going.

ROB. It'll be back.

CLARA. Nora says she wants to put the house up for sale.

ROB. And what do you say?

CLARA. This house eats money.

ROB. You can afford it.

CLARA. I don't want it. I don't even want to stay the night here. It's full of –

ROB. I'm listening.

CLARA. When Mum got sick Harry bought every device he could find that might improve the life she had left. Electric hoist on the stairs, hospital rails on the walls, ramps for the wheelchair. I remember Harry saying it was the first time he'd noticed he was really rich. He said whatever he did, she was going to die way before he could spend all the money. And now she's gone, they're both gone and it's just the machines left, all the stuff he bought, that didn't – that failed to – prolong her life. This is their place, where they always were and now they're not and it's just – It's too hard. I keep thinking, why won't he just walk in now? Why won't he just walk in?

I don't know. (*Shrugs.*) Bury the dead. Isn't that what they say?

ROB. What do you say?

Silence from CLARA.

Apparently you consider me too frivolous to deal with these grim realities.

Still nothing from CLARA.

You know, maybe I'm secretly tired of being scorned as a cheery fool while the rest of you grown-ups go around being serious.

Enter DANNY, *carrying a tray of sandwiches which he places on the table beside* ROB*'s book.*

DANNY. Good book?

ROB. Biography of Hitler.

DANNY. Interesting read, is it?

ROB. He dies in the end.

Enter NORA, *with more tea.* DANNY *gets up to help her.*

DANNY. You look tired.

NORA. I am tired.

CLARA. Sit down, for chrissakes, Nora.

NORA. There's another plate of sandwiches in the kitchen.

DANNY. I'll go.

NORA. Thanks. (DANNY *exits.*)

ROB. Nora, I think we have enough sandwiches now. Truly.

CLARA. Did you make these?

NORA. No. Are they nice?

CLARA (*chewing*). No. (*Taking another one.*) What's in the boxes?

NORA. Oh. It's all things from the shed. Harry's shed. I was looking for – you know how he hoarded everything. Letters, cards, travel tickets, theatre programmes. I remember once he showed me a napkin from the restaurant they were in when mum told him her idea for Colin, and she drew rabbits all over the napkins to show him. I knew he kept all this stuff, folded away somewhere and I thought it was probably in that ancient cupboard with the feet.

CLARA. That huge battered wooden thing with all the drawers.

NORA. He used to hide presents in there. That walking talking doll for my birthday when I was six.

CLARA. My goldfish. That time we went to the fair and I really wanted to win a goldfish and I hit all the balls into the net but they gave me this horrible enormous pink bear.

NORA. Which was the highest prize.

CLARA. But I really wanted the goldfish. I cried all the way home. The next day Harry brought me into the shed and opened a drawer and there was a goldfish, swimming in a green plastic bag. I called him Roger.

NORA. They always left us something, when they went away. A note, a game, that map once, to find the treasure hidden in the garden before they got home.

CLARA. It took us six days.

ROB. What was the treasure?

NORA (*shrugs, looks to* CLARA). Do you remember?

CLARA. No. I just remember where it was. It was buried under Arthur. (*Goes over to a particular gnome, clearly a special gnome. The head gnome.*)

NORA. I never touched that shed while Harry was alive. And then, three days ago, I went in. I imagined reading it all, their letters, the whole story. I was telling myself, even, to go through them slowly, not to use them up too quickly. And I got there and I opened the chest and I went through every drawer and they were all empty.

CLARA. Maybe it's all under here, hey, Arthur? (*Checks.*) Anything? Nope.

ROB (*rummaging in the boxes*). How many souvenirs does a person need? (*Brings out two rabbit hand puppets.*)

NORA. There was a tape, I found this tape, of Harry reading – but I can't make it – work – (*While speaking, she's pressed the 'Play' button on the little stereo. They listen to the crackle for a second. CLARA turns it off, again, abruptly.*)

CLARA. I asked Mum once, did she keep Harry's letters to her, and she just laughed. She said, 'I threw away the letters and I kept your father.' (CLARA*'s mobile rings, she answers it.*) Hello. Speaking. Who? No comment. I have no comment. Where did you get this number? Fucking tabloid scum. Planting photographers in hedges trying to get a shot of a TV starlet with no make-up on while real news happens elsewhere. I'm at MY FATHER'S FUNERAL, you fat fuck. AND THANK YOU SO MUCH FOR YOUR KIND WISHES AT THIS TIME. (*Hangs up. Pause. She looks at* NORA, *opens the newspaper at the relevant page.*) I don't know where they get their information.

NORA. Is it true?

CLARA. What do you think?

ROB (*examining the paper*). I think you could do better. The man has very pronounced jowls.

NORA. Are you getting married?

CLARA. Are you serious?

ROB. Are you going to answer the question?

NORA. I didn't know what to think. I tried to phone you. I left you seven messages. You never called me back.

CLARA. Am I supposed to apologise now?

ROB. In your own time.

CLARA. Did you really think I'd get married and not tell you?

NORA. I was worried about you.

CLARA. Nora. Jesus. You shouldn't be so nice to me.

NORA. Why not?

CLARA. I know you didn't like him.

NORA. I didn't know him. I met him twice. I thought he was a bit – feral. He looked at you the way you'd look at a very expensive chocolate truffle.

CLARA. He likes women.

ROB. He likes getting married. You would have been his fifth wife.

CLARA. And he's on perfectly amicable terms with all of them. Including the children. Two with his first wife, one with his second, twins with the third, and two with the fourth. Sort of a family for each decade.

NORA. I never really understood what he *did*.

CLARA. For his money? Nothing. Inherited it. Johnny's biggest problem was thinking of ways to spend it all. He collected a lot of art.

ROB. He collected things that were hard to get.

NORA. It's not funny.

CLARA. Don't worry. My days as a plaything are numbered. Even my agent's starting to lie about my age. Anyway, I make enough money to buy my own art. I'll be fine. I have my nice job, and my nice car and my nice life, and while I'm waiting for my happy ending maybe I'll get myself a small manageable dog who'll sit at my feet and love me unconditionally.

NORA. I never know when you're joking.

CLARA. I only joke about serious things.

NORA. He just didn't seem – Well, like a serious person.

CLARA. Ah. What's a serious person? Do I seem like a serious person?

ROB. We always take you seriously.

NORA. I wish – it's just – you don't tell me what goes on. I asked you once if you were in love with Johnny and you said, 'Well, he has very beautiful clothes.'

CLARA. Well. Love.

DANNY enters with more sandwiches. CLARA takes one and eats it.

(*To* DANNY.) Did you make these?

DANNY (*nodding, agreeing*). Good, aren't they?

CLARA. Your Americans used up all the hot water. How many of them *are* there, anyway?

NORA. Six. They wash a lot.

ROB. Very clean nation. White-collar America, three showers a day on average. Either they're very concerned about hygiene or they feel guilty about something.

DANNY. They're taking advantage. Nora gives them four sausages each for breakfast, d'you know what I mean? Fuckin' scones and cream and three kinds of milk and new towels every day. Tea and sandwiches when they come in, tea and sandwiches when they go out. You can't run a business that way. (*To* NORA.) Babe, you are as sweet as they come but you've the financial acumen of a bag of hammers.

ROB. Maybe you could give her a few tips.

DANNY. She could do worse.

ROB. Yeah. I read your brochure.

DANNY. It's what people want now. Supply and demand.

CLARA. What are you supplying, exactly?

DANNY. It's a retreat. Exactly what it says on the tin. Peace. Time out. Find your own meaning.

ROB. I'd rather someone else found it for me.

DANNY. This country's changed. You can have it all, but then what? Richest generation in history, all they do is cry about it. Biggest growth industry is books telling them why they're so unhappy.

CLARA. What do you sell the people who have everything?

ROB. Short breaks with God.

DANNY. We prefer the word *spiritual*.

ROB. Oh. God is optional.

CLARA. Unfashionable.

DANNY. Call it what you like. It's the right idea at the right time. My old da used to say, success is fifty per cent timing.

ROB. What's the other fifty per cent?

DANNY. Ah, talent, planning, good luck, I dunno.

CLARA. Your old da sold cars that didn't work.

DANNY. Yeah. OK. My old man wasn't much. To you. He sold cars. He had some bad luck.

CLARA. He was a liar.

DANNY. He made things bigger than they were.

CLARA. He made himself bigger than he was.

DANNY. He was a storyteller.

CLARA. He was a liar and a cheat.

DANNY. Who isn't? He had the gift. Like Harry. When you're rich and mighty it's all fuckin' *charming* and *eccentric*. Harry's the Great Man, National Treasure. My dad, he's just a liar. At the end of the day, Harry, my dad, they both liked to make believe the world was a bit different than it is, y'know? Pull back the curtain and it's the fuckin' Wizard of

Oz, just another ordinary scared little guy pulling the strings, pretending he's magic.

ROB. There are worse things than being ordinary.

CLARA. Not if you want to be magic.

NORA. Harry never cheated anyone.

DANNY. Listen. People cheat themselves. They're always looking for a shortcut. Something's wrong with your life, you're not going to fix it with a week in the country doing yoga. But everyone's looking for a deal. They see what they want to see. There's no deals. There's no bargains. You get what you pay for. I believe that. They want to come out in the country, find some peace and and call it God, good luck to them.

ROB. But you don't believe in God.

DANNY. You know what it's like? The trains on the London Underground. They all have drivers at the front, right? But the drivers don't drive the trains. They just open and close the doors. The trains are driven by a computer somewhere. What's the driver there for? They're there because people feel happier seeing someone up front, *looking like* they're driving the train. D'you know what I mean?

ROB. Ah, it's a parable. Just like Jesus.

DANNY. Time like this, you have to be thinking about the future. Me and Nora – (DANNY*'s phone rings, he answers it.*) Yeah, I'll call you later. Yeah. Later. (*He hangs up.*) Yeah – where was I – ?

ROB. You and Nora. The future.

DANNY. You have to know what you want.

CLARA. And what does Nora want?

NORA. Maybe you should *ask Nora.*

CLARA*'s mobile phone rings, she answers it.*

CLARA. Hello? Oh, not again, for FUCKSAKE! (*She hangs up, throws phone on ground and stalks offstage.*)

DANNY. Happy fuckin' families, huh?

ROB. You know any?

JACK *enters, with* RUBY *behind.*

JACK. I can come back later.

NORA. No, no. Come and sit down.

CLARA *comes back in.*

ROB (*who now has the phone. Throwing it to* CLARA). Looking for this?

CLARA (*catching the phone, goes to* JACK). We haven't met. I'm Clara, Nora's sister.

JACK. Pleased to meet you.

NORA. Everyone, this is Frank McBurney, who's in charge of the funeral service. This is Clara, and Rob, who's a very old friend.

ROB (*shaking hands*). But everyone says I look great for my age.

JACK. Call me Jack.

NORA. I'm sorry, I thought, the woman who answers the phone in your office, I thought she called you Frank.

JACK. She probably did. In fact, she probably called me *Poor Frank.* (*Shaking hands with* DANNY.) Dan.

DANNY. Howareyou, Jack?

ROB. You know each other?

JACK. We went to school together.

DANNY. Until they threw me out.

CLARA. Bet you've got some stories.

RUBY. Every undertaker in the world's got stories.

DANNY. I heard about the – well. I'm sorry for your loss, man.

JACK. I think that's my line.

RUBY. A lot of stories they can't tell.

CLARA (*shaking hands*). I'm sorry, is it *Frank* or *Jack?*

DANNY. He was Frank at school. The first day the teacher read out the class list, there was a misprint or something –

JACK. I was down as Jack Jack. The teacher – I can't remember her name –

DANNY. Mrs Craven. Face like an cow's arse.

JACK. She said. 'Ah. (DANNY *joins in.*) Jack Jack. So good they named you twice.' Big Sinatra fan. By the end of Mixed Infants we could all sing *My Way.*

DANNY. He was always Frank after that.

JACK. It's a small town.

RUBY (*joining in*). . . . small town.

DANNY. D'you fancy a sandwich? Cup of tea?

JACK. Thanks.

CLARA. Can we just –

JACK. Of course. (ROB *offers a cigarette,* JACK *takes it, lights* ROB's *and his own. He takes out his notepad. There's a listening silence.*) Right. Well. I'll take you through all the options. Basically, it depends what you want. Burial or cremation.

NORA (*quickly, unilaterally*). Burial.

RUBY (*joining in*). Burial.

JACK. Right. OK. Then the casket.

DANNY. Y'know, I was thinking about that. Like, do we have to buy a whole – eh – casket? It's not like we need the full size – d'you know what I mean?

He becomes aware of what he said. The others just look at him, combination of disbelief and disgust. They ignore him.

CLARA. Do you have a – brochure or something we could look at?

RUBY. Who'd be an undertaker? In a town like this.

JACK (*brings out brochure which* CLARA *takes and starts to read*). We do, of course.

RUBY. They'll call you out in the middle of the night, sure, but who wants to run into you afterwards, on the street, the guy who buried their husband, their sister, their best friend?

JACK. We carry everything from a plain pine box, or cardboard even, eco-friendly, no fuss, inexpensive, up to caskets in better wood – oak, mahogany. Carved or plain.

RUBY. Nothing personal, but you don't get invited to many parties.

JACK. Or metal caskets. Steel, copper, bronze. Whatever you want.

CLARA. Is there a difference between a coffin and a casket?

RUBY. No.

JACK. Coffins are usually wooden and narrower. Caskets are rectangular – they have some – extra features. But basically – basically they are the same thing.

ROB. I like *casket*. It sounds more –

CLARA. Expensive.

ROB. I was going to say important.

CLARA (*studying the brochure*). There really are a bewildering number of options. We could have a box with the Last Supper painted on it. A box with red satin cushions, a box with heaven on the lid. Handcarved box made of imported wood, probably comes with its own choir of angels.

RUBY. It's not the box that makes it expensive.

CLARA. It says these are unsealed.

RUBY. It's what's inside the box.

NORA. What does that mean?

JACK. Sealing is this protective rubber along the rim of the casket that prevents moisture and air from entering. That's mostly available with the metal caskets. The most expensive wooden caskets will not last as long as the most inexpensive metal.

RUBY. Some people are very interested in lasting.

CLARA. What do you advise?

JACK. I don't. Different things are important to different people. How people feel is their own business. To some people it's very important the casket should be sealed, to other people it's irrelevant. They're both right. No-one should have to explain why it matters or why it doesn't matter.

DANNY. In prehistoric times when the dead started to smell the family just moved to the next cave. I read that somewhere.

CLARA. Great business opportunity here, Daniel. Despite extraordinary technological advances, people just keep on dying. It's a sure thing. Supply and demand.

NORA. I don't think this is –

CLARA. Brochure carries the full price range, but you can be quite confident that *really*, your customers, whether they feel sad or guilty or desperate or just lost, well – they're standing in front of a stranger and they're damned well not going to choose to bury their dead *in public* in a cheap plywood box with the lid screwed down. Betcha. Nine times out of ten.

JACK. People aren't stupid. The most expensive casket in the world won't make up for abuse or neglect. The cheapest box can't hide real grief.

RUBY. Or love.

CLARA (*to* JACK). What would *you* bury *your* father in?

RUBY. Or your wife?

JACK. We buried him in Number 24.

RUBY. It's on page eight.

Small pause while CLARA *finds Number 24 on page eight.*

CLARA. Well. That seems fine. That looks splendid. (*Shows it to* NORA, *who just nods.*)

JACK. So that just leaves the service. Burial usually means – a church service.

RUBY. In this town.

NORA. I'm not sure –

RUBY. Local church looks like the foyer of a bank.

JACK. I don't know how you feel about a church service.

RUBY. You've probably walked past it a hundred times and not noticed it's a church.

CLARA. Let's leave God out of it.

ROB. An increasingly popular choice.

RUBY. Place always looks closed.

NORA. Harry was an agnostic.

ROB. Never say never.

CLARA. He didn't believe in *churches.*

RUBY. At my funeral, they had to leave the doors open –

NORA. I don't know –

RUBY. It was June and everybody was sweating in their good suits.

NORA. I don't know what he'd want.

RUBY. Priest got my name wrong.

NORA. Clara?

RUBY. Fair enough. I hadn't set foot in a church for years.

JACK. With a cremation, you can have a different kind of service. Have friends, family get up and talk about the person who died.

RUBY. No-one spoke for me.

CLARA. He's dead, Nora. He doesn't want anything, he can't approve of anything anymore. You can't do anything for him, or to him. He's just a bunch of things we remember or we've forgotten or we made up.

RUBY. All that priest knew was that I was twenty-nine.

CLARA. Funerals are to console the living. It's your party.

RUBY. Snapped open his Bible, gave a stirring recruitment drive.

CLARA. If you need to warm your hands at some fluffy soft-focus tribute evening, that's fine. Don't pretend it has anything to do with what Harry wanted.

RUBY. She's right.

NORA. I didn't know you felt like this.

CLARA. You didn't ask.

RUBY. It doesn't matter what the dead want.

NORA. I just thought –

CLARA. WHAT?

NORA. I thought we needed an ending.

RUBY (*joining in*). . . . an ending.

CLARA. Tidy it up?

RUBY. Call it what you like.

ROB. That should appeal to you, Clarabelle.

CLARA (*to* NORA). We GOT an ending. We got Mum dying in eighteen months of a disease lots of people survive for years. One day she's walking, the next she's falling down. Two months later she can't hold a pencil. She can't get up the stairs. Six months, she can't feed herself. She can't stay upright on the toilet. She can't talk. They have to operate to keep her from drowning in her own spit. Harry flying in one expensive second opinion after another and they're all the same bloody opinion. Drugs that make her hair fall out, drugs that make her put on so much weight we nearly can't

recognise her, drugs that don't do anything at all. Homeo-
paths, herbalists, acupuncture, fucking FAITH HEALERS.
Harry, who never believed in anything he couldn't see,
he buys her that machine, the voice-simulator she could
operate just by lifting her eyebrow, and all I hear now when
I try and remember her voice is that awful robot voice
asking us to kill her. She's dead a year and they find Harry's
car, a shoe by the cliff. Months of policemen and questions.
'Did we have any reason to believe he did it on purpose?
Any reason at all.' In the last five years you've been seven
times to the mortuary to identify bodies that aren't his. On
and on and on until I end up on some TV special, poignant
little fucking celebrity postergirl for the families of Missing
People. All their terrible terrible hope that keeps them going
year after year when they can't bury their dead. All their
will and imagination and all their wishes for the next year
and the next used up on the one thing that can't happen.
There were forty families on that programme and not one
happy ending. They're still waiting. I felt like a total fucking
fraud. I went home and cried. Not because I couldn't recover
from Harry's death, but because I *can*. It IS FINISHED. You
want to make it sweeter? You want a happy ending? Make
your own. I'll miss them forever but that story's over.
What's left of Harry is not in that box. It's not IN THAT
HOUSE. For *you* I will go to your party and I'll stand by
the hole in the ground and I'll watch them all watching me
to see if I cry and I won't say another word about it. Just
don't ask me to get excited about what words we use on
the headstone.

Pause.

ROB (*to* JACK). I bet you hear a lot of stuff people never think
they want to say.

JACK. No. I think they want to say it.

NORA (*to* JACK). I'm sorry.

JACK. What for?

NORA *makes an apologetic gesture. She nervously plays
with the tape; it crackles and plays the first bit again, as*

before, before DANNY *puts his hand over hers, stops the tape.*

NORA. It's silly, I can't make it – play.

DANNY. Give it to me. (NORA *is reluctant.*) C'mon, babe, give it to me. I'll see if I can fix it. I'll fix it for you. I promise. C'mon. (*She hands it over.*)

NORA. We had a happy childhood. Here. In this house.

CLARA. We did have a happy childhood. It was lovely. I'm thirty-five. You can't sit in your happy childhood polishing the bloody memorabilia forever.

NORA. I'm not.

CLARA. What *are* you doing then? Pretending to run a B&B, washing towels and re-arranging the exhibits in this fucking mausoleum. Every time I hear you, your voice has gotten quieter. You've been wearing that same pair of jeans for five years. I'm looking at you and I'm thinking I don't know what a happy childhood equips people for.

DANNY. That's a bit rough now.

CLARA (*to* DANNY). Was I talking to you?

DANNY. I don't think you should talk to Nora like that.

CLARA. Would it surprise you to hear that I DO NOT CARE what you think? What are you even doing here?

DANNY. I've a right to be here.

NORA. He's part of this family. Harry –

CLARA. Harry is dead. You are under no obligation to babysit his collection of lame ducks forever.

DANNY. I'm Nora's husband.

CLARA. Everyone makes mistakes.

DANNY. She's not like you.

CLARA (*to* NORA). It's like you're *asleep.*

DANNY. She's loyal. Faithful.

ROB. Fidelity should not always be taken personally.

CLARA. Loyal. Yeah, Nora's loyal as a fucking dog. A dog
that licks its owners hand after he's kicked it with his boot.

NORA. Stop it. (*She turns to* ROB.)

CLARA. Don't look to Robert to get his hands dirty. He's been
sitting on the fence so long he fucking broke it.

DANNY (*turning away, to* NORA, *puts his arm round her*).
Shouldn't mix the red pills with the blue pills, y'know,
Clara.

CLARA. Don't touch her.

DANNY. You don't tell me what to do here.

ROB. OK. That's enough.

CLARA. Speak for yourself.

ROB. I do my best.

CLARA (*to* DANNY). Since the black day Nora married you,
I've been sticking pins in your effigy hoping you'd just
fucking drop dead.

DANNY. There was a time, I remember, there was a time you
found me pretty fucking convenient –

CLARA. I look at you and I see bruises on her arms. I look at
you and I hear her crying and crying in the night. I look at
you and I see her *disappearing.*

DANNY. I look at you and I see a liar. Riding in on your high
horse. You judge me but I look at you and I see you five
years ago. Calling me in the middle of the night when you
couldn't get your dealer on the phone. 'Danny, could you
please, just this once, Danny – ' Begging me. Fuckin'
begging me.

CLARA. Fuck you.

DANNY. Oh, you would've. If it would've got you what you
wanted. What you needed. You offered. I was just scared
what I might catch.

CLARA *hits* DANNY.

(*Laughs.*) Yeah. Yeah. The truth hurts.

NORA *sits down, carefully.* CLARA *starts to go towards her. They look at each other.* CLARA *leaves.* DANNY *and* ROB *stand either side of* NORA. *They look at each other, dangerously.* DANNY *is the one to leave, kicking a box out of his way. He knocks it over, it spills several Colin the Rabbits onto the ground.* ROB *comes to* NORA. *He touches her head.*

ROB. Nora?

NORA *shrugs him off.*

OK. OK. Just promise me this, beautiful. You will not volunteer to carry every cross. People who carry crosses get crucified.

He leaves the stage. NORA *is left alone except for* JACK *and behind him,* RUBY, *standing forgotten off to one side. She crosses to the box with the spilled rabbits. She sits, sets the box back upright, and starts to put the rabbits back. Instead, she switches one of the rabbits on. It hops around horribly on the floor. She just sits, watching it hopping around.* JACK *comes to stand next to her and kneels down beside her. The lights fade.*

Blackout.

Interval.

ACT THREE

Scene One

The next morning. NORA *and* CLARA *are in the garden. The table is littered with glasses and mugs that no-one has cleared. There is probably fresh tea. They are just sitting, not talking.*

NORA. Are you cold?

CLARA. I'm fine.

NORA. D'you want my jacket?

CLARA. No.

NORA. I don't need it.

CLARA. I'm fine.

Silence again. NORA *takes off her jacket and goes and puts it over* CLARA'*s shoulders.*

For chrissakes.

Shrugs off the jacket. It falls on the grass. More silence. They sit. Eventually CLARA *picks up the jacket and puts it on. She says, very quietly:*

Thanks.

Enter DANNY. CLARA *glares at him, he glares back. He sits down. She gets up, leaves.* NORA *sighs.*

DANNY. Did you sleep out here?

NORA. I didn't sleep.

DANNY. I'm not going to say I'm sorry.

NORA. That makes two of you.

DANNY. Your sister's a fucking lunatic.

NORA. She's upset.

DANNY. She's hysterical.

NORA. She needs a bit of time.

DANNY. She needs a good slap.

NORA. Do you think so?

DANNY (*pause*). That was a long time ago. (*Another pause.*) People change, y'know. They change. They're not one, one, flavour their whole fuckin' life, Nora.

NORA. Maybe.

DANNY. You're different. I'm different.

NORA. We're just older.

DANNY. I've known you since you were fifteen.

NORA. What was I like then?

DANNY. Kind. Pretty. I dunno. Quiet.

NORA. And what am I like now?

DANNY. Is this a test or something? Fuck, I know you. I'm married to you for Jesus' sake.

NORA. You're married to me on some bit of paper. Before yesterday I hadn't spoken to you for three years.

DANNY. You're my family, Nora.

NORA. I don't think I have a family anymore. Harry made this family. Without him we're just, I don't know, a collection of people who know each other, up to a point.

DANNY. We can make our own family. You always said you wanted a baby. We'd have a good-looking baby, you and me. You'd be an excellent mother, Nora, I'd be nearly fuckin' jealous of any baby has you as its mother. Till I remembered who it's daddy was, eh? (*Laughs.* NORA *doesn't laugh.*) Let's do it. If that's what – Why not?

NORA. Danny.

DANNY. Yeah.

NORA. I don't want to have your baby.

DANNY (*pause*). Right. (*Pause.*) Was it so bad? Was I so fucking bad to you?

NORA. Sometimes.

DANNY. You loved me.

NORA. I did.

DANNY. We were happy.

NORA. Sometimes.

DANNY. You regret it?

NORA. Sometimes.

DANNY. But not always.

NORA. But not always.

> CLARA *enters. She stares at* DANNY, *who doesn't move. Eventually he gets up.*

DANNY (*to* NORA). I'll see you later.

NORA. The cremation is at five.

DANNY. I'll meet you there. (*Exits.*)

CLARA. What cremation?

NORA. Change of plans.

CLARA. Why?

NORA. Isn't that what you wanted?

CLARA. What do you want?

NORA. I want – You know, if you'd asked me last week, yesterday even, I might have said, I wanted you to ask me, I just wanted you to ask me that. I want, I don't know – I want to get amnesia and not know who I am and start again. I want not to believe I have bad luck. I want to shout at people who still have their mothers and fathers and aren't grateful. I want Danny to feel sorry that he doesn't love me, properly, that he hasn't – I want him to know he's missed something. I want us to be a family. I want a clean slate, I want a real life. I want to leave this house. I want to leave this house.

CLARA. We are a family.

NORA. You left.

CLARA. Someone had to.

NORA. They missed you.

CLARA. I couldn't just hide out here in the bloody enchanted forest forever.

NORA. You ran away.

CLARA. I grew up.

NORA. I missed you.

CLARA. I'm here now. Let's not – I'm *here now.*

CLARA *reaches a hand out to* NORA, *who takes it briefly.*

Is that what you're wearing?

NORA. Yes. No. I'll – go and get dressed. (*She exits.*)

CLARA *is left sitting, on the grass, outside. Her mobile rings. She has beside her one of the boxes and a pile of papers, letters. She looks up distracted, to answer it.*

CLARA. Phone. I mean, hello . . . If you're looking for Nora, she went back up to the house.

ROB *appears, phone held to his ear. He hangs up.* CLARA *also hangs up, puts phone down.*

ROB. I'm not looking for Nora. (*Standing where he came in, not moving.*) Are you crying? (*Starts moving towards her.*)

CLARA. I don't want to talk about it.

ROB. I didn't ask. (*Makes one of the bunnies hop around near her.*) C'mon. Don't cry. Look, cute bunny. Cute bunny does tricks.

CLARA. That is not a cute bunny. That's Colin the Rabbit failed Christmas merchandise from 1978. They were withdrawn after complaints that they frightened children.

ROB. That's my girl. (*Hands her a tissue.*)

CLARA. That thing is not clean. I'd rather blow my nose on my sleeve, thanks.

ROB. I haven't seen you cry since you were fifteen.

CLARA. I cry all the time. I don't cry in front of people.

ROB. OK.

CLARA. I wanted to help. To help Nora.

ROB. There's a lot of that about.

CLARA. I just wanted to help.

ROB. They should never have sent you to the Brownies, darlin'.

CLARA. I was never in the Brownies. I was in the Legion of Mary.

ROB. OK. (*Lights cigarette, one for her first.*)

CLARA. We used to empty our collection boxes and switch all the silver money to coppers and use the profits to buy sweets.

ROB. I won't tell a soul.

CLARA. I hate Danny. I hate him. He's a lowlife unrepentant scum-sucking piece of shit.

ROB. Yep. He's nearly a country-and-western song all by himself.

CLARA. He's the fucking heart of darkness.

ROB. Maybe.

CLARA. Maybe?

ROB. Danny didn't put the needle in your arm. Did he?

CLARA. I never used needles.

ROB. Did you call him in the middle of the night?

CLARA (*pause*). Yes. Yes. You know it's true, what he said. I forgot a lot of things that happened when I was using, but not that. That's all true.

ROB. I know.

CLARA. How do you know?

ROB. Danny is not good at keeping secrets.

CLARA. I didn't want you to know.

ROB. Because I wouldn't like you anymore?

CLARA. You never said anything.

ROB. I was waiting for you.

CLARA. Why didn't you say something?

ROB. I was waiting for you.

CLARA. Are you angry with me?

ROB. No.

CLARA. Nora's angry with me.

ROB. I think you're angry with you.

CLARA. I have a therapist already, thanks.

ROB. Good.

CLARA. What are you doing here?

ROB. I just wanted to make sure you hadn't run away to sea.

CLARA. I didn't know you cared.

ROB. Yes you did.

CLARA. Are we having one of those conversations where everything means something else?

ROB. I thought you liked those.

CLARA. I need a drink.

ROB *passes her some wine. She drinks.*

ROB. Does it make it all go away?

CLARA. Y'know, alcohol never did anything for me. Drugs, on the other hand – The first time I tried heroin I knew it was the thing for me. For the first time, the first time, I looked at myself in the mirror and I didn't want anything, it was – *I was* – enough. I didn't need attention or work or sex or God or money or anything except myself, I was just – peaceful. My mother used to say you should make yourself content *within yourself* before you look for anything else, and it suddenly made perfect, beautiful sense. I loved myself, I loved what I could do, everything I needed was in my own hands. It lasted about an hour but it was more powerful, more – just *more* than anything before. Or anything since. My therapist says it's possible to achieve contentment without mind-altering substances, but, y'know, she's paid to say that. So. Back to square one.

ROB. I think the only people who truly don't want anything are dead.

CLARA. I want too much. I want things I can't have. I want to fall asleep in the back of a car on the way home, my parents in front, laughing in the dark and me and Nora safe and loved and at the beginning of everything. I want to wake up and look forward to the day. I want to feel hopeful. I want to believe that people mean well.

ROB. I want to hit Danny.

CLARA. I want to tell you, I want to tell you – I want to go back five years. Five years ago when you woke up beside me with this look. This look like an animal caught in a trap who's prepared to chew off its own leg if it will help it escape.

ROB. Did I look like that?

CLARA. That is the wrong answer.

ROB. I'm sorry if I looked like that. I didn't feel – How do I look now? How do I look now?

He pulls her into a kiss.

Blackout.

Scene Two

It's late afternoon, the sun going down. JACK *is sitting
waiting, at the table which has been cleared of the empty
glasses, mugs, etc. from last night/this morning.* RUBY *is
sitting near him/behind him as usual. He is reading a book.
Beside him is a plastic urn, containing Harry's ashes.*

RUBY (*reading out the title of the book* JACK *is reading*).
'Teach Yourself Greek.'

JACK. Why not? I've never been anywhere. I've never been on
a plane or further than England.

RUBY. I know.

JACK. Last week. I went into Eamon at the travel agency, to
talk to him about his mother, she's up in the hospital, her
fifth stroke, they don't expect her to come home, he wants
to talk about arrangements. I go in and there's a young
couple in before me, expensive-looking, Eamon's talking to
them, so I wait. They're looking for round-the-world tickets.
They're flicking through all the brochures, and the girl looks
really bored. She says to Eamon: 'You see, we've *been* to
most of these places *already*.' Eamon says: 'Well, if you've
used up the rest of the world, there's always Tibet.' She
says: 'Is that in Europe?' They leave without buying the
tickets, Eamon turns to me and says: 'Third-level education.
Wasted on the fuckin' middle classes.' Next customer comes
in as we're talking, looks about the same age as the Bored
Girl, but she's carrying a baby in a sling and another one
clinging to her knee. She has about ten shopping bags that
all spill out round her feet when she sits down. She wants to
price a fortnight by the sea. I'm thinking there's a caravan
park twenty miles down the road after Bundoran but you
can see she just wants to get as far away as she can afford,
which isn't very far. Even Scotland is too expensive. She's
emptying her handbag onto the table. In the end Eamon
finds her something decent in Antrim. She shakes both our
hands leaving and forgets her shopping. After I left Eamon
I remembered I'd seen that girl before, she's married to

Charlie Conway now, they live out near the mountains on
his parents' farm, but she used go round all the houses on
Saturdays, with a bunch of other schoolkids, offering to
wash your car for a pound. That wasn't so long ago. Four
years maybe. I was thinking about that and I was thinking
I'd like to learn a foreign language. So. Are you laughing
at me?

Long pause, in which it seems like RUBY *isn't going to
answer and* JACK *goes back to his book.*

RUBY. No.

NORA enters.

NORA. No sign of Rob and Clara. I thought they were
following us in the car.

JACK (*puts his book down, pushes a chair out for her, next to
him*). They'll be along in a minute.

NORA (*looking at the book cover*). Are you going to Greece?

JACK (*shrugs*). I also bought *Teach Yourself Italian* and
Croatian For Beginners.

NORA. You like to travel?

JACK. I don't know. I never did.

NORA. My favourite bit was always coming home.

JACK. You, and the guy who wrote this. Listen to his list of
useful phrases, at the back:

'*How much money did you have in your handbag?*

It's quieter here.

I saw them stealing it.

Prices were cheaper last year.

I cannot hear you very well.'

JACK / NORA (*joining in, reading over his shoulder*).
'*My room is small.*

I missed the bus.

I don't like this colour.

This town is not as interesting as the last one.'

NORA. Aren't there any happy ones?

JACK (*reading*). 'Ask the policeman over there.

We need a bigger room.

He left yesterday.'

NORA (*laughs*). It's Italian for people who don't want to go there.

JACK. My mother said to me once, when she was quite old, that she'd never seen a bus or a train pull out of the station without wishing she was on it.

NORA. Did she ever get to travel?

JACK. After my father died, she went out to New Zealand to visit my sister.

NORA. And did she enjoy that?

JACK. She's still there.

NORA (*checks watch*). You must be wanting to get home.

JACK. Don't worry about that.

NORA. Thank you for – arranging this.

JACK. That's my job.

NORA. I wouldn't have known what the legal – what you can do?

JACK. You can dispose of a person's ashes anywhere. In most cases you can bury someone in their own back garden if that's what they want.

NORA. You've been very patient with us.

JACK. That's my job.

NORA. Changing our minds at the last minute.

JACK. Customer's always right.

NORA. Clara was right. I think she was right. About the cremation. I think that's what Harry would have wanted.

JACK (*gently*). I think Clara is right that funerals are for the living.

JACK *offers* NORA *a cigarette, lights it for her. He notices something on her wrist as she takes the cigarette. He touches her wrist.*

NORA. Oh, that's just – these red spots, they just appeared. These horrible red bumps that itch and burn in the night. The doctor said it was an allergy – d'you think it might be something in the garden?

JACK. No.

NORA. Or washing powder. I was thinking it might be this new brand of washing powder I used.

JACK. I think it might be grief.

NORA. I've been trying to remember Harry properly, but every time, every time I try and think about his life all I end up thinking about is how he died.

JACK. It said in the papers he was out walking and he fell. It said the Guards were not treating it as a suspicious death.

NORA. He didn't leave any note. So, we don't know. We say we don't know. I wasn't living here then. My mother was dead a year, not even a year, and Harry was living here on his own.

It was a Tuesday night, two policemen turned up on my doorstep. I thought it was something to do with Danny. But they said they'd found Dad's car, it had been sitting there for days, in the car park near the cliffs. He liked to walk there. He used to say he'd like a memorial bench there one day, with a plaque. Anyway. They found his shoe. Down, on the rocks. They said it wasn't conclusive. They called me every now and then, when a body washed up there. For five years, it wasn't him. I don't think he meant us to have to wait five years. I suppose no-one around here thinks he fell.

JACK. Who cares what they think. What do you think?

NORA. When my mother died, the day of her funeral, I found
   him in their bathroom clearing out all her drugs and
   medicines. The sink was full of all these coloured plastic
   bottles, he said the doctor had told him to bring some of
   them back to the hospital, they were expensive and they
   could be used again. He said he was just thinking about
   someone else taking these pills that had already failed once.
   And I saw that his face had changed, it had this – blurred
   look. He'd never looked old to me before. His face never
   changed back. He never – got over it. He never even tried.
   He still talked to her.

   After that. After that I talked to him every day on the phone
   and I thought it was a bad line, his voice had gone so soft,
   like he was always talking from the next room. He spent
   a lot of time sleeping. When I did come to the house he
   drove me mad because he couldn't make up his mind about
   anything: what to eat, what to wear, when to do things.
   His hands shook. It took him half an hour to make one
   cup of tea. He'd sort of wander about uncertainly like the
   arrangement of the rooms was always surprising him. One
   day he was chopping up a tomato for dinner and he cut his
   hand. He just stood there, all the blood dripping onto the
   floor. And I was so *angry* with him. That he was suddenly
   so – dithering and – and incompetent. This was my dad,
   who was a fixer, who could mend anything, who always
   knew what to do. If you held his hand you felt safe in a
   strange city, in a bad neighbourhood, on a dark country road
   without a map.

   The doctor came and said there was nothing medically
   wrong with him. He was very fucking jolly about it. He
   said, 'It comes to us all, hohoho.'

   I think a lot about that day he drove to the cliff. What was
   he thinking? Was there some sign I should have noticed?
   There were two hundred thousand bloody signs. And, was
   there anything we could have done, to prevent it, what
   happened, what he did? *Yes.* Yes.

JACK. That will drive you mad. My wife was killed ten yards
   from our house. We usually met on our way home. That day

I stopped to buy a donut from the Spar. I was hungry. I'd missed lunch. I thought about that a lot. I thought about it for four years. Then I had to stop thinking about it.

NORA. I wanted to say. I've been wanting to say, I was so sorry about your wife. I wanted to send a card. I thought you were probably getting lots of cards and letters you wouldn't even want to read. I didn't know would you really remember me.

JACK. I remember you.

NORA. I knew her to see, but I'd never talked to her. I don't think I knew her name.

RUBY. Ruby.

JACK. Ruby.

NORA. Do you mind talking about it – her?

RUBY. Do you?

JACK (*pause*). Not any more.

NORA. I suppose everyone asks you about it.

JACK. Actually, no-one talks to me about it at all. They talk to each other about it. Half the town probably think I killed her and got away with it. The other half think it's very tragic, so now I'm very tragic and they're just waiting for me to kill myself. For two years they looked surprised every day I showed up for work. They never found the car that hit her. I sat in that police station for two days without a lawyer. They kept asking me about Ruby, about our marriage. I told them we had a good marriage. One of them, he just smiled when I said that.

RUBY. He had this wet, red mouth and when he smiled it made his mouth smaller.

JACK. He said: 'No-one has a good marriage.'

NORA. When I said I was getting married, Rob tried to talk me out of it. He said: 'People don't start out wanting to make each other unhappy but that's how it always ends up.' (*She has come back to the B&B sign and is tugging at it.*)

The B&B – I think I just wanted the house to be full of people again, to be *used*. When I moved back here all my friends said they'd definitely come and visit, they couldn't wait to get out of the city, breathe clean air, eat good food –

JACK. See you. (*He gets up to join her, standing on the other side of the sign.*)

NORA. See me. Yeah. Well. I think two of them came, once. And, you know, I don't even like breakfast. (JACK *starts pulling it out from the other side.*) I can manage.

JACK. But you don't have to.

NORA. Because my parents had a good marriage – I think Clara and I took it for granted, that that was how married people were. We had high expectations. (JACK *removes it and lays it face down on the ground beside them.*) Thank you.

JACK. I think you should expect good things for yourself. There are good surprises as well as bad. (*He reaches behind* NORA*'s ear and produces a playing card.*)

NORA (*laughing, and this might be the first time she's really laughed*). How did you do that?

JACK *shrugs, reaches behind her other ear and produces a flower. While this is going on* RUBY *has moved from beside/behind* JACK *to behind* NORA *and for one moment she is sharply illuminated and she and* JACK *look directly at each other. This moment is interrupted by* CLARA *and* ROB, *who enter together.*

ROB. I got rid of the Yanks. I told them the heating broke down and sent them to Mrs McSorley at the Welcome Inn.

NORA. Thank you.

ROB. They dug up a bit of the garden as they were leaving and put it in a bag to take home. They're going to frame it or something.

CLARA *pulls a jumper on and lights a cigarette. It's getting darker and colder in the garden as the sun disappears.*

CLARA. So. What now?

NORA. Danny's not here yet.

ROB (*looking at his watch*). It's getting dark.

JACK. Let's wait a few minutes.

There's a bit of general pacing around. CLARA *goes over to the urn.*

CLARA. Is this – ?

NORA. Harry. Yes.

ROB. Does Danny know to come here?

NORA. I left a message. He was supposed to come to the place, the crematorium.

CLARA. Let's just start.

NORA. Wait a few minutes.

ROB. It's getting dark.

NORA. OK. OK.

She hands CLARA *a small spade,* CLARA *digs a hole.* JACK *brings the urn and places it in the hole.* NORA *and* CLARA *throw earth on top of it. They wait, looking at it. It's evening now, the sun has all gone and during the last part of this scene the gnomes begin to light up, as if on a timer, randomly, one by one, until they are finally all lit and glowing.*

(*To* CLARA.) D'you want to say something?

CLARA (*pause*). No. (*Pause.*) No. I don't think so.

RUBY. I want to say something.

CLARA (*to* NORA). Do you? (NORA *shakes her head.*)

RUBY. There's an old poem, maybe it's a ballad or something.

CLARA (*to* JACK). We should thank you –

RUBY. A girl dies and her true love puts her in the ground.

JACK. You did.

CLARA. You mean, Nora did.

RUBY. He puts her in the ground but he can't get over it and he sits by her grave –

JACK. No, please –

RUBY. He sits by her grave every day for a year. A year passes –

CLARA. You've been very – kind.

RUBY. – A whole year passes and he's still there and the dead girl rises from her grave and begins to speak.

JACK. No –

NORA (*to* JACK). You have.

RUBY. She says: 'Who's sitting here crying over me, who won't let me sleep?' And, she doesn't look like he remembers her. Of course. Because she's dead.

JACK. I remember –

CLARA. I'm sorry – ?

RUBY. October 29th. You turned the corner for home and you saw –

JACK. I remember –

RUBY. Glass and blood on the road. My mouth was open. And my eyes. You picked up my shoe from the grass.

NORA. Jack?

RUBY. A mile down the post office road. A sunny day. Three letters in your hand that you never posted. You closed my eyes.

JACK. I'm sorry.

RUBY. Why are you sorry?

ROB. Everyone's sorry today.

RUBY. She says, the girl in the poem, she says: 'You can cry over me forever but you'll never kiss me again. Never, unless you join me in the grave.'

NORA. Jack? Are you all right?

RUBY. Because the dead never really come back and the living
live on and sooner or later – sooner or later –

JACK. No. (*Pause.*) I'm OK. I'm fine.

ROB. In Mexico they have a Day of the Dead. Families cook
a special meal for their loved ones who have died and leave
a place for them at the table. They lay a trail of flower petals
from the grave to their table so the dead can find their way
to the food they've prepared.

RUBY. Or so they can find their way back.

CLARA. They do it every year?

NORA. I like that.

ROB. Depends how you feel about ghosts.

    DANNY *enters.*

DANNY. Howdy, folks.

NORA (*to* DANNY). Where were you?

DANNY. Yeah, look, I'm sorry. Car broke down and I couldn't
get there in time. Piece of shit car. Had to leave it on the
road, hitch back.

NORA. Where were you?

DANNY. Had to meet someone. I thought I'd make it back,
easy. How'd it go?

CLARA. It was a blast.

DANNY (*indicating the freshly dug hole, etc.*). What's all this?

NORA. We're burying the ashes. We cremated Harry and now
we're burying his ashes. Where were you?

DANNY. I said, I'm sorry.

NORA. Where were you?

DANNY. I had to meet someone. It's not important.

NORA. How can you say it's not important?

DANNY. I meant – Look, the car broke down. I'm sorry and all but there it is. The fucking car broke down. Act of God. All right?

CLARA. No.

DANNY. Nora. I said I'm sorry. I'm sorry. I'm fucking sorry. I'm sorry. I'M SORRY . . . Nora?

NORA. Let's just. Please. Just –

DANNY. Look. Nora. Look. I was meeting someone. I was meeting someone, right? The car broke down. I tried to get here and the fucking car broke down, I said I'm sorry. I'm here now, right. I'm here now.

CLARA. Who were you meeting?

DANNY (*to* NORA). What's it fucking matter who, for fuck's sake?

NORA. It doesn't. It doesn't. (*Takes out a cigarette, tries to light it, lighter keeps clicking, empty.* DANNY *takes out his lighter and lights her cigarette.*)

DANNY. Nora.

NORA *doesn't respond.*

Ah, what the fuck d'you want me here for anyway? Mess up your private party by saying the wrong thing. But I knew your parents, I was there, and fuck you if you don't like to remember me messing up your cosy little family picture. Here's what I remember, I remember when your ma was really sick, nearly at the end, and they were arguing over whether to put her on the ventilator and she didn't want to. And she couldn't hardly move at all, you had to lift her fingers onto the computer mouse for that speaking machine. I was sitting with her one afternoon, reading to her, and I thought she was asleep, but she started clicking the mouse and the voice came out of the speakers, that weird jerky robot voice like the speaking clock, all weird stops and starts while she found the right word on the computer. She was talking about Harry, about how she still fancied him, and she still wanted him, wasn't that strange, her body all

wrecked as it was, but she could still feel *that*. There. She
said it was the one thing left. She said maybe it sounded
sick or perverted or vulgar to me, but it was wonderful and
she wanted to tell someone. She said it was wonderful. That
he still wanted to fuck her even now – *she* said that, those
words – even in this state, old and sick and broken, and that
she was *so grateful*. She said she was staying alive for that.
Y'know there was a lot of talk about how the disease was
affecting her brain and she was liable to say things that
weren't, that she didn't mean, but this was real. This was real
and I thought it was beautiful – well. That's it. I don't have
a letter or a poem or some clever fuckin' quote you all know
what it means and it makes everyone cry. I'll leave yous to it.
Wouldn't want to dirty up the – the proceedings cause
I haven't read the right *books*.

There's a long pause.

ROB. Yeah. That's a wrap.

NORA *moves to touch* DANNY *on the arm, he shrugs her
off.*

DANNY. I said I was sorry.

ROB. Amongst other things.

DANNY. You asked me to come.

NORA. I thought you'd want to be here.

DANNY. I came, didn't I?

NORA. If not for me, then for Harry.

DANNY. Look. I showed up. I paid my respects. I loved Harry
    and Margaret, they were good people, they were good to
    me. I'm grateful. How long d'you want me to go on crying
    over what's finished and ended? Your parents die before
    you, Nora, that's the natural order, read the fucking small
    print. What d'you want from me?

NORA. Nothing.

DANNY. Yeah.

NORA. I'm going to sell the house.

DANNY. Whatever you want, Nora. Do whatever you want.
Just do something.

NORA. That's what I want.

DANNY. Fine. I've got to get going.

NORA. Now?

DANNY (*shrugs*). I've got the keys to my brother's place.

NORA. Well.

DANNY. I don't have a car. Left mine in the road, I hitched
back here.

NORA (*gets out her car keys and gives them to him*). Take
mine.

DANNY (*pause, then takes them*). I'll call you. Right? Nora?
I'll call you.

NORA. Yeah.

DANNY (*long pause*). Here. (*Takes out a tape from his pocket
and hands it to* NORA.)

NORA. What is it?

DANNY. Your tape. Harry's tape. I fixed it. I took it to this guy
I know and – well, anyway. It's fixed now. So. I'll call you.
We'll. Yeah. I'll call you.

He exits, leaving NORA *holding the tape. She turns it over,
examining it.*

By now, all the gnomes are lit. ROB *goes over to the table,
opens a bottle.*

ROB. Is there a bottle opener around here?

NORA (*opening a bottle*). Screw top.

CLARA. And more wine –

NORA. Crates of it. Up at the house.

JACK. I'll go. (*Exits.*)

ROB. I think we need a toast.

CLARA. Shouldn't you be getting home to your naked Australian?

ROB. Annie? Annie lives in my house. That's all. She just lives in my house.

CLARA. Why?

ROB. She needed somewhere to live.

CLARA. You're not fucking her?

ROB. I am not fucking her.

CLARA. Why?

ROB. She's not interested in me.

NORA *has started to laugh.*

Yeah, it's a mystery to me too.

CLARA. But you want to fuck her.

ROB. No.

CLARA. But why? When she looks so lovely naked and all.

ROB. Maybe I'm getting too old to be fooling around with one woman when I'm in love with another.

CLARA. You're never too old for that.

ROB. We've been here before.

CLARA. We have been here before. I lose a parent, you roll up, looking sensitive, we have sex, then you fuck off to Eastern Europe.

ROB. It was Guatemala. I had a job.

CLARA. I had a job too. I was waiting for you to phone me.

ROB. Yeah. I know. I was waiting for me to phone you. I'm sorry.

CLARA. Well.

ROB. People change. Some of them even improve. (*Pause.*) I read in the papers you were moving to Hollywood. Star in a remake of *Gone With The Wind.*

CLARA. Dunno where they got that from. It's a B-movie about a tunnel exploding. I'm a feisty single mother with unexpected construction expertise. I think I die at the end but I get to save New York City first. I might even get my name above the credits this time. Their people are talking to my people.

ROB. New York.

CLARA. New York.

ROB. It's a wonderful town.

CLARA. Will you miss me?

ROB. Is that a trick question?

CLARA. Will you miss me?

ROB. You want it in writing? I will miss you. I'll call you in the middle of the night and sing *After You Gone* to your answering service. When I wake up in the morning I'll think about how my bed is enormous and empty and decide to adopt a kitten although I'm allergic to cat hair and responsibility. I'll go to the corner shop in my pyjamas and think how since you left what is there to get up for, except biscuits? I'll suffer mild existential angst in coffee shops and light my cigarette from the wrong end. I'll tell everyone I meet how life lost its meaning since you went away to Hollywood and took the instruction manual with you. I'll treasure the – socks – and other memorabilia you left in my house. I'll start writing poetry about it.

CLARA. Yeah, but will you miss me?

ROB (*pause*). Yes.

CLARA. Come with me.

ROB. We'll visit.

CLARA. I'll send you a ticket.

ROB. I'll send you a ticket.

CLARA. I'll send you a ticket. I can afford to buy five hundred bloody tickets.

ROB. But this will be *my* ticket.

CLARA. I'll drink to that.

ROB. Let's all drink to that. Have a drink, Nora. Have two.

NORA. Where did Jack go?

ROB (*to* CLARA). Where did Jack go?

CLARA. Did he?

ROB. I'm going to New York.

NORA. So I hear.

JACK (*just re-entered, carrying bottles of wine*). That's nice.

CLARA. Isn't it?

JACK. Were you looking for me?

CLARA. There he is.

ROB (*relieving him of the bottles*). Good man.

NORA. I thought you'd gone.

JACK (*to* NORA). No.

> ROB *opens more wine and offers glasses to* NORA *and* JACK.

NORA. Thank you. (*Sits down, realises she's sitting on something, takes the tape* DANNY *gave her out of her pocket, looks at the tape, turning it over in her hand reading something written on it.*)

CLARA. What's that?

NORA. Danny gave it to me.

ROB. Nice of him.

CLARA (*taking the tape from* NORA *and examining it*). It just has the date on it.

ROB. Is he coming back, d'you think?

NORA. No.

CLARA. Well –

NORA. Don't say it.

CLARA. What?

NORA. Whatever you were going to say.

CLARA. It might have been a nice thing.

ROB. Yeah. It might.

JACK. It's a fine night, though.

ROB. It is.

CLARA. It is.

RUBY. It is.

NORA. It is.

ROB. A toast: to Harry and Margaret.

Everyone lifts their glasses. ROB *notices* JACK *is toasting with a glass of water.*

You don't drink?

JACK. I used to.

CLARA. Isn't it bad luck or something to drink a toast with water?

JACK. I don't believe in bad luck.

ROB. To Harry and Margaret.

CLARA. Harry and Margaret.

NORA / JACK / RUBY. Harry and Margaret.

They drink. NORA *lifts her glass again.*

NORA. And – to Ruby.

CLARA. Who's Ruby?

JACK. My wife.

NORA. Ruby.

CLARA (*raises glass*). Ruby.

ROB. Ruby.

They drink raising their glass towards JACK. *A pause.*

(*Raising his glass again.*) And – to the gnomes. An astonishing collection. Surely no class of gnome is unrepresented. I wish I'd asked Harry *why* he was collecting them, but nonetheless, an extraordinary achievement.

NORA / CLARA / JACK. The gnomes.

JACK. I was just remembering. One year I came home for Christmas, I was living in the city then. I drove into town and all over the main street and most of the side streets there were these big handwritten signs, 'Happy Birthday Maggie', everywhere, bus stops, shop windows, on the library gates, the entrance to the Esso station. When I got home I asked my father and he said it was your mother's fiftieth birthday and Harry had recruited half the town, to help him get it ready for when your mother came into town to do her shopping.

NORA. He did things like that. Big gestures.

CLARA. He was probably apologising for something.

ROB. D'you remember our graduation day? It was raining and Harry had a huge black umbrella and he kept offering it to my Aunt Sylvia and she kept politely refusing and getting wetter and wetter until eventually he just stood behind us and held it over her. In the car afterwards she kept saying: 'Who was that man? Do I know him?'

NORA. He used to write back personally to every single child who sent him a fan letter about Colin the Rabbit.

CLARA. He was great with *children*.

NORA. When our tortoise died he told us it was just sleeping.

CLARA. For two years. And Nora believed him.

NORA. I thought he knew everything.

CLARA. He knew why the sky is blue and why the earth isn't flat and how to throw a ball and how to make the best ham and mustard sandwich you ever tasted. He never once said 'I don't know.' He never said some things are unfair, some lives are too short, some burdens are too great, some love just – ends.

NORA. It took him half an hour to get down the street sometimes, he'd say hello to everyone and have a chat. He was so concerned always, that people around him were *all right.* He always thought he could fix it.

CLARA. You can't repair everything.

ROB. He wanted to protect you.

CLARA. He didn't.

JACK. He couldn't.

ROB. Well said. So, what's next?

CLARA. What do we *drink* to next?

ROB. If you like.

NORA. The future?

ROB. I'm too old to be looking forward to my future the whole time. All that longing and practising in front of the mirror and next thing you know it's all over and someone's calling it the best years of your life. I'll drink to the present moment.

JACK. Eight thirty five.

CLARA. Shall we synchronise our watches?

NORA. We're not so old.

ROB. Thank you. One day, *one day*, we'll be old, and – immobilised by fear of death. We'll watch TV all day and wear slippers. We won't understand the currency. We'll stop young people on the street and ask them why they're going about dressed in their underwear. We'll forget what we had for lunch an hour after we had it, but we will remember this.

CLARA. Maybe we'll remember it differently.

ROB. Remember what you like. As long as you enjoy it. As long as you're awake. As long as you're not hankering after what came before or what happens next.

CLARA. I have no idea what you just said but I'm willing to drink to it anyway. To whatever he said.

NORA. What are you doing? (ROB *has taken out a camera and is pointing it at things.*)

ROB. Capturing the moment. When when we're old and tired, won't it be nice to have this cheery record of our youth, our optimism, our friendship –

CLARA. How we looked with teeth.

ROB. Nore, are there any more sandwiches?

JACK produces some chocolate from his pocket and offers it around.

NORA. No.

ROB. Thank God.

CLARA (*chewing*). Lovely.

ROB (*picking up the tape that* DANNY *gave* NORA). Was this a parting gift?

NORA. I suppose so.

ROB finds the tape recorder and starts to play the tape. There's about a minute of heavy crackling, distortion, in which we recognise the tape that NORA *was trying to play earlier.*

ROB. I think this might be Side Two.

ROB looks up when CLARA *says:*

CLARA. Why did Danny give you a tape?

NORA. He gave me it back. It's that one of Harry, of Harry reading.

ROB. What, he fixed it?

NORA. I think so.

CLARA. I'm really hungry.

NORA. It's so pretty out here.

CLARA. I think something bit me.

ROB (*trying the tape, which hisses but no voice is audible*). I can't hear anything.

NORA. But I don't want to spend another night here.

JACK. Are you leaving?

CLARA. We're selling it. Are you interested?

JACK. I don't think so.

CLARA. We'd give you a good price.

JACK. I've been thinking of moving on myself.

NORA. Where would you go?

JACK. I don't know yet.

  NORA *and* JACK *look at each other*

CLARA. OK, I'm cold now.

ROB. Take my jacket.

CLARA. Cold *and* hungry.

ROB. I think that's my cue. (*He gets up, helps* CLARA *up.*)

CLARA. We could get some food at that place on the corner, the Green something.

JACK. The Green Tree.

CLARA. Nora?

NORA. Yeah.

ROB. You ready?

NORA. Yeah, I think so. (*She looks around the garden. Takes a long look around and turns to go.*)

CLARA. What?

NORA. Nothing.

JACK. Ready?

NORA. Ready.

She turns to go, and as she turns finally, she knocks over Arthur, the gnome, whose light goes out. As Arthur breaks definitively the other gnome lights start sputtering and failing and going out, one by one or in groups so the light is dimming fast. The effect is that of the whole garden being dismantled.

CLARA. Ready.

ROB. Are you sure? You don't want to smash any more gnomes or anything – because – y'know, there's plenty left here – look –

CLARA (*leading him away forcibly*). C'mon.

He follows CLARA offstage, taking CLARA's hand, CLARA already holding NORA's. JACK is onstage briefly after the others leave and he and RUBY look at each other. As RUBY speaks, the last of the gnomes are still going out until the stage is quite dim and only she and JACK are lit for her last words. The tape machine is still crackling in the background, forgotten.

RUBY. For our fifth anniversary you were going to give me a piece of the moon. It turns out it is actually possible to own a piece of the moon. In 1980 a man called Dennis M. Hope claimed the entire moon. He just filed a claim for it with the US and USSR governments. I didn't know they owned the moon. Now you can buy an acre of the moon's surface from a catalogue.

Almost everything that belonged to me is gone from our house. But in the left front drawer of the dresser in the kitchen there is a piece of paper with the exact location of my acre of the moon.

You can survive the thing that happens to you. You will not be permanently undone by grief. But regret. Regret will kill you if the cigarettes don't get there first.

As the man said: 'Forgetting me, remember me.'

NORA *comes back for* JACK.

JACK. Yeah. (*Pause.*) Yeah. The dead must be buried. Sooner or later. (*He turns away from* RUBY *and he and* NORA *exit together.*)

RUBY. For the sake of the living. For the sake of the living, the dead must be buried.

The tape is still crackling as it has been since ROB *put it on. The lights dim to a tiny spot on* RUBY *as she moves over to the tape machine. As she moves towards it,* HARRY'S VOICE *comes clear, telling the last bit of a 'Colin the Rabbit' story. The light dwindles as the tape plays, until only the tape machine is lit:*

HARRY'S VOICE. ' . . . It had been a very long and confusing day, thought Colin, and he was very tired. He remembered a thing his Uncle Balaclava used to say, before he got so cross and stopped speaking to people altogether. His uncle used to say: 'We live in complicated times.' Colin had asked his mother what this meant and his mother just said: 'You'll understand when you're older.' She said this every time Colin asked her anything interesting. Tonight Colin felt a great deal older and tireder than he had felt this morning when he found the ring inside the fish and met the strange and beautiful blind white rabbit who had told him he was going to go on a long journey full of surprises. Back home now, safe and warm in his own bed, Colin really didn't feel that he wanted any more surprises. 'Goodnight,' said Colin's mother. 'Goodnight,' said Colin, falling asleep. He would worry about all that tomorrow.'

Apparently the end of the recording, a long hiss/crackle of distortion/old tape and then a voice cuts in.

TECHIE'S VOICE. D'you want to run that again, H?

HARRY'S VOICE. No. No, I think that's fine now. That'll do fine. Yes. Thank you.

Blackout.

The End.

A Nick Hern Book

Words of Advice for Young People first published in Great Britain
as a paperback original in 2004 by Nick Hern Books Limited,
14 Larden Road, London W3 7ST in association with
Rough Magic Theatre Company

Words of Advice for Young People copyright © 2004
Ioanna Anderson

Ioanna Anderson has asserted her right to be identified as
the author of this work

Cover image: Alphabet Soup

Typeset by Country Setting, Kingsdown, Kent CT14 8ES
Printed and bound in Great Britain by Bookmarque, Croydon,
Surrey

A CIP catalogue record for this book is available from
the British Library

ISBN 1 85459 798 1

Amateur Performing Rights   Applications for performance,
including readings and excerpts, by amateurs in English should
be addressed to the Performing Rights Manager, Nick Hern Books,
14 Larden Road, London W3 7ST, *fax* +44 (0)20 8735 0250,
e-mail info@nickhernbooks.demon.co.uk, except as follows:

Australia: Dominie Drama, 8 Cross Street, Brookvale 2100,
fax (2) 9905 5209, *e-mail* dominie@dominie.com.au

New Zealand: Play Bureau, PO Box 420, New Plymouth,
fax (6) 753 2150, *e-mail* play.bureau.nz@xtra.co.nz

Professional Performing Rights   Applications for performance
by professionals in any medium and in any language throughout the
world should be addressed to Nick Hern Books, 14 Larden Road,
London W3 7ST, *fax* +44 (0)20 8735 0250, *e-mail*
info@nickhernbooks.demon.co.uk

No performance of any kind may be given unless a licence has
been obtained. Applications should be made before rehearsals
begin. Publication of this play does not necessarily indicate its
availability for amateur performance.